NATIONAL GEOGRAPHIC KiDS

weird but true!

STICKER DOODLE BOOK

This book belongs to:

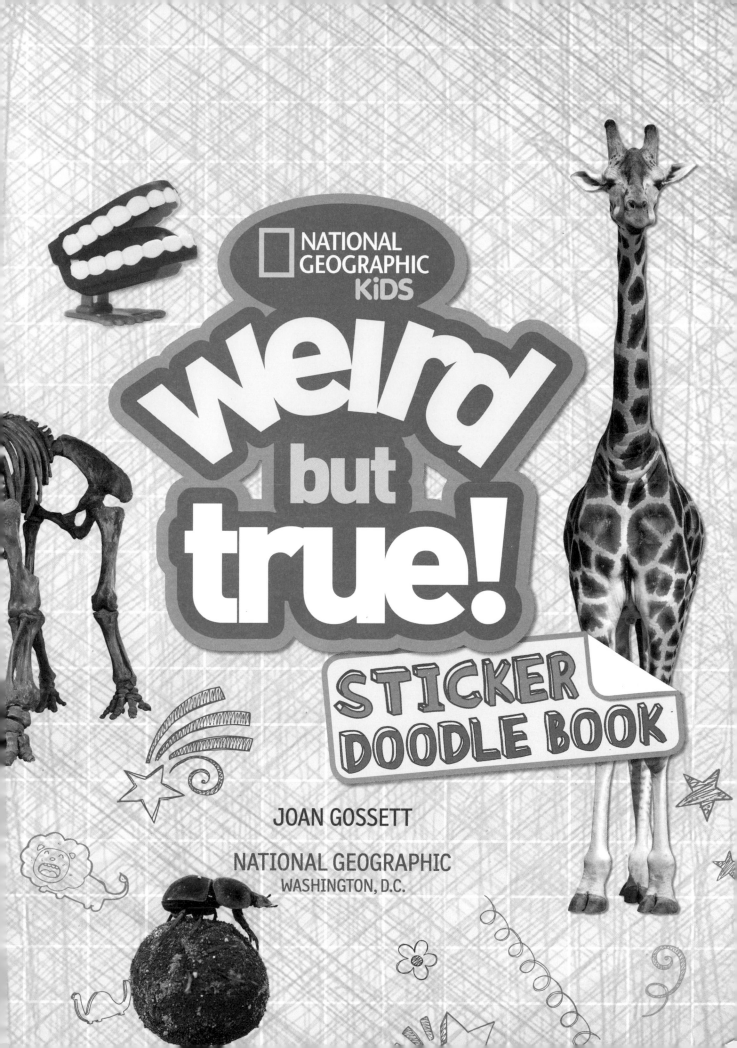

NATIONAL GEOGRAPHIC KiDS

weird but true!

STICKER DOODLE BOOK

JOAN GOSSETT

NATIONAL GEOGRAPHIC
WASHINGTON, D.C.

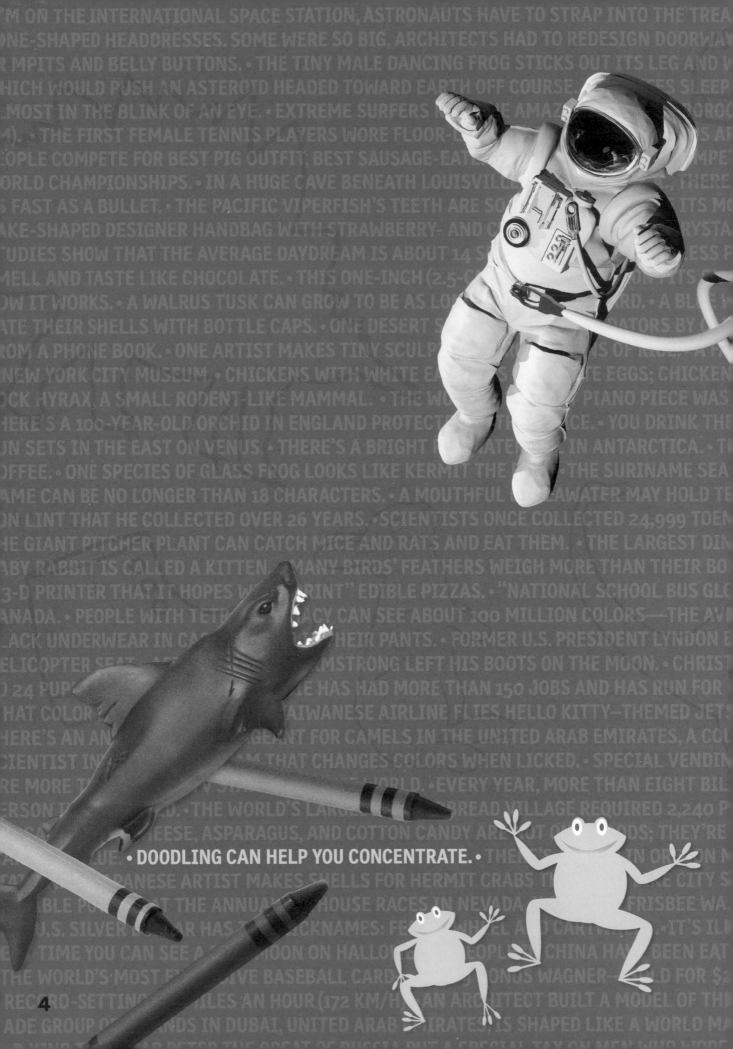

M ON THE INTERNATIONAL SPACE STATION, ASTRONAUTS HAVE TO STRAP INTO THE TREA
ONE-SHAPED HEADDRESSES. SOME WERE SO BIG, ARCHITECTS HAD TO REDESIGN DOORWA
R MPITS AND BELLY BUTTONS. • THE TINY MALE DANCING FROG STICKS OUT ITS LEG AND K
HICH WOULD PUSH AN ASTEROID HEADED TOWARD EARTH OFF COURSE
LMOST IN THE BLINK OF AN EYE. • EXTREME SURFERS
4). • THE FIRST FEMALE TENNIS PLAYERS WORE FLOOR-
OPLE COMPETE FOR BEST PIG OUTFIT, BEST SAUSAGE-EAT
ORLD CHAMPIONSHIPS. • IN A HUGE CAVE BENEATH LOUISVILLE
S FAST AS A BULLET. • THE PACIFIC VIPERFISH'S TEETH ARE SO
AKE-SHAPED DESIGNER HANDBAG WITH STRAWBERRY- AND C
UDIES SHOW THAT THE AVERAGE DAYDREAM IS ABOUT 14 S
MELL AND TASTE LIKE CHOCOLATE. • THIS ONE-INCH (2.5-C
OW IT WORKS. • A WALRUS TUSK CAN GROW TO BE AS LO
ATE THEIR SHELLS WITH BOTTLE CAPS. • ONE DESERT S
ROM A PHONE BOOK. • ONE ARTIST MAKES TINY SCULP
NEW YORK CITY MUSEUM. • CHICKENS WITH WHITE EA
OCK HYRAX, A SMALL RODENT-LIKE MAMMAL. • THE W
HERE'S A 100-YEAR-OLD ORCHID IN ENGLAND PROTECT
N SETS IN THE EAST ON VENUS • THERE'S A BRIGHT
OFFEE. • ONE SPECIES OF GLASS FROG LOOKS LIKE KERMIT THE
AME CAN BE NO LONGER THAN 18 CHARACTERS. • A MOUTHFUL
N LINT THAT HE COLLECTED OVER 26 YEARS. • SCIENTISTS ONCE COLLECTED 24,999 TOEN
HE GIANT PITCHER PLANT CAN CATCH MICE AND RATS AND EAT THEM. • THE LARGEST DIN
ABY RABBIT IS CALLED A KITTEN MANY BIRDS' FEATHERS WEIGH MORE THAN THEIR BO
3-D PRINTER THAT IT HOPES W RINT" EDIBLE PIZZAS. • "NATIONAL SCHOOL BUS GLO
ANADA. • PEOPLE WITH TET ACY CAN SEE ABOUT 100 MILLION COLORS—THE AV
LACK UNDERWEAR IN CA HEIR PANTS. • FORMER U.S. PRESIDENT LYNDON B
ELICOPTER SEAT MSTRONG LEFT HIS BOOTS ON THE MOON. • CHRIST
0 24 PUP E HAS HAD MORE THAN 150 JOBS AND HAS RUN FOR
HAT COLOR AIWANESE AIRLINE FLIES HELLO KITTY—THEMED JET
HERE'S AN AN GEANT FOR CAMELS IN THE UNITED ARAB EMIRATES, A COU
CIENTIST IN M THAT CHANGES COLORS WHEN LICKED. • SPECIAL VENDIN
RE MORE T ORLD. • EVERY YEAR, MORE THAN EIGHT BIL
ERSON I D. • THE WORLD'S LARGE PREAD VILLAGE REQUIRED 2,240 P
EESE, ASPARAGUS, AND COTTON CANDY ARE T CO RDS; THEY'R

• **DOODLING CAN HELP YOU CONCENTRATE.** •

PANESE ARTIST MAKES SHELLS FOR HERMIT CRABS 1 E CITY S
BLE PO AT THE ANNUA HOUSE RACES IN NEVADA FRISBEE WA
U.S. SILVER AR HAS ICKNAMES: FE HAEL AND CART W IT'S IL
TIME YOU CAN SEE A OON ON HALLO EOPL CHINA HA BEEN EAT
THE WORLD'S MOST E IVE BASEBALL CARD ONDS WAGNER D FOR $
ECORD-SETTING ILES AN HOUR (172 KM/H AN ARCHITECT BUILT A MODEL OF TH
ADE GROUP O NDS IN DUBAI, UNITED ARAB IRATES, IS SHAPED LIKE A WORLD

4

How to Use This Book

Welcome to the wild world of **Weird But True!** In this book, you'll find wonderfully weird facts about nature, space, sports, history, food, fashion, and so much more. And just as you're soaking in each fact—wondering how weird, awesome, gross, cute, or funny it is—you'll be invited to unleash your imagination, creativity, and brainpower by way of **doodles, mazes, puzzles,** and lots of other activities that will take you from weirdness to whimsy in 0 to 60! **Cryptograms** and connect-the-dots, **wacky word scrambles** and **funny fill-ins,** crazy quizzes and **brain games**—you'll find them all in this book. Awesome photographs accompany the facts, bringing them to life. **We set the scene for you,** and you fill in the rest!

Let's get started! You don't have to begin at the beginning. Dip your toe into the middle or jump all the way to the end—anywhere you choose. Make sure you have some crayons, markers, or colored pencils, and a regular pencil or pen. If you need help with answers, you'll find them at the end of the book. And don't forget to use the 150 weird and wacky stickers provided to add to the fun.

Not weird but definitely true: You'll have a blast with this **fun-tastic book!**

Scientists discovered a **prehistoric animal** shaped like a **balloon** and covered with **spines.**

That would have made a cool pet. What would you name it? What would it eat? Draw your perfect pet.

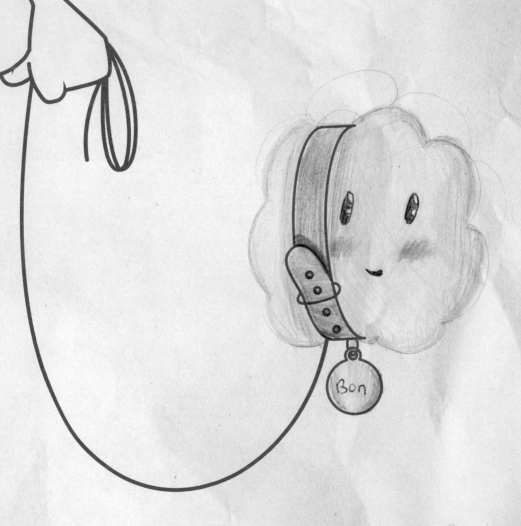

If an octopus **loses** an arm, the **limb** will continue to **hunt** for food.

Uh-oh, these animals are missing something, too. Help them out by completing the drawings. Be sure to color them when you're done!

A walrus tusk can grow to

be as **long** as a **Boogie board.**

Walruses use those long tusks to pull themselves along the ocean floor, sliding on their stomachs. Draw yourself slipping and sliding in the sea with a herd of walruses!

A life-size
LEGO FOREST
was once set up in the Australian outback.

Dear _____

_____

_____

_____

_____

_____

_____

_____

_____

_____

_____

_____

_____

_____

Write a persuasive letter that will convince your principal to set up a Lego display at your school. Attach your own design of the display.

Sincerely,

Scientists can **make cheese** with **bacteria** from armpits and belly buttons.

What's growing in your belly button?
What are your bacteria up to? Have they built an itty-bitty town in there?

One **French town** holds an **annual pig festival,** where people compete for **best pig outfit,** **best sausage-eater,** and **best squeal.**

These pigs need some funny outfits!

The tiny male
DANCING FROG
sticks out its leg
and waves its foot
to attract a mate.

That sounds like a dance move! Imagine a frog dance party. **They'll need some party hats.**

In **BELGIUM**, there are **POSTAGE STAMPS** that **SMELL AND TASTE LIKE CHOCOLATE.**

Create a stamp about something that's special to you. It doesn't have to smell like anything. But you could rub or spray the paper with something that smells good.

In the **gym** on the **International Space Station,** astronauts have to **strap into the treadmill** and bike so they **don't float away.**

There's no gravity weighing you down in space, so go ahead and lift that heavy barbell! Design some exercises and equipment for your anti-gravity gym. You'll need some space workout clothes, too.

Some scientists want to build a **giant space "tractor"** that would **push an asteroid** headed toward **Earth** off course.

Scientists keep an eye on asteroids and comets and study their orbits to see if they will come near Earth. If you had to, how would you stop an asteroid?

Bonus Activity!
Grab an adult and go online to download NASA's "Asteroid Watch Widget," which lists the biggest asteroids expected to come the closest to Earth. But don't worry—"closest" means 4.6 million miles (7.4 million km) away—or 19.5 times the distance from Earth to the moon! Find out more at *nasa.gov/asteroid-and-comet-watch*.

A **CAVE** in Croatia has a **1,683**-FOOT-DEEP **PIT,** the **DEEPEST HOLE** on Earth.

(513-m)

Time to go spelunking! Wind your way through this maze on your cave expedition.

START

FINISH

SOME **DOGS' NOSES** TURN FROM **BLACK** TO **PINK** IN COLD WEATHER.

Color these noses any color you like! Then finish the drawings.

The first **female tennis players** wore **floor-length dresses.**

The International Tennis Foundation wants you to *design tennis uniforms* for the next championship!

In a **huge cave** beneath Louisville, Kentucky, U.S.A., there's an **extreme bike park, as big as six football fields.**

You've just been asked to design your own awesome underground city, park, or attraction! What will it be?

Competitors **hurl their old cell phones for sport** at Finland's annual **Mobile Phone Throwing World Championships.**

Don't throw your phone—or anyone's! Instead, design a cool protective case and matching selfie stick for this smartphone. Add some phone charms and other bling!

The Pacific viperfish's **TEETH ARE SO BIG,** it can't close its mouth.

Sounds like this fish needs to make a trip to the orthodontist! Outfit these fish with braces, rubber bands, and retainers.

The arctic tern's round-trip migration is about 44,000 miles, (71,000 km) the longest of any animal.

Its wings must get tired! Grab a map or globe and unscramble the names of these points on its migratory route.

GALNEREDN

IATARTCANC

APCE REEDV NSSILDA

NHTOR TIACLTAN CNOAE

NORTH AMERICA

Breeding grounds

Southward route

AFRICA

Northward route

SOUTH AMERICA

Wintering grounds

Bonus Activity!
The information about the arctic tern's migration was discovered in a first ever study using tiny tracking devices attached to the birds to follow their migration! For more information, grab an adult and go online to *arctictern.info*.

Researchers are developing clothing that will GENERATE POWER as the wearer moves.

Ask a friend to give you words to fill in the blanks in this futuristic story without showing it to him or her. Then read out loud for a laugh.

TOP SECRET

The year is 2050, and I'm on my way to school. It's a little chilly, so I'm wearing a light _____ . I hear the bell, so I start to
item of clothing

_____ . Then I remember I'm wearing my power
verb

_____ , and before I know it, I'm _____ ! A(n)
piece of clothing   *verb ending in -ing*

_____ and a(n) _____ pass me. I see _____ ,
noun   *noun*   *place*

so I turn in that direction. Then a strong _____ bumps against
noun

me, spinning me in circles. Now where am I? Up ahead, I see a(n)

_____ _____ taking off; I recognize the local airport.
adjective   *noun*

The tower is ahead. I _____ toward it, but I'm _____
verb   *verb ending in -ing*

so fast, I go right by. I can see the looks on the faces of the

_____ . I manage to slow down and make a U-turn. This
profession, plural

time, I reach out and _____ on to the point of the tower. I
verb

spin several times, but I hold on tight. I see a(n) _____ racing
noun

toward the tower. The rescuers raise a long _____ and I climb
noun

on, then make my way down the _____ . I'm safe. But I'm very
noun

late for school—and I don't have a note!

20

There's a
100-year-old
orchid
in England **protected**
by the **police.**

What will this little seed grow into?
Draw and color your plant.
Don't forget to use your green thumb!

Some
PLANTS
communicate
with one
another.

*Make your own
knock-knock joke!*

Knock, knock.

Who's there?

Wooden.

Wooden who?

**Wooden you like to make
some jokes with me?**

Knock, knock.

Who's there?

_____

_____

_____

_____

_____

_____

SEEDS

The **closest living relative** of the **elephant** is the **rock hyrax,** a small rodent-like mammal.

This elephant and hyrax are meeting each other for the first time on national TV! What do you think they'll say to each other?

LIVE

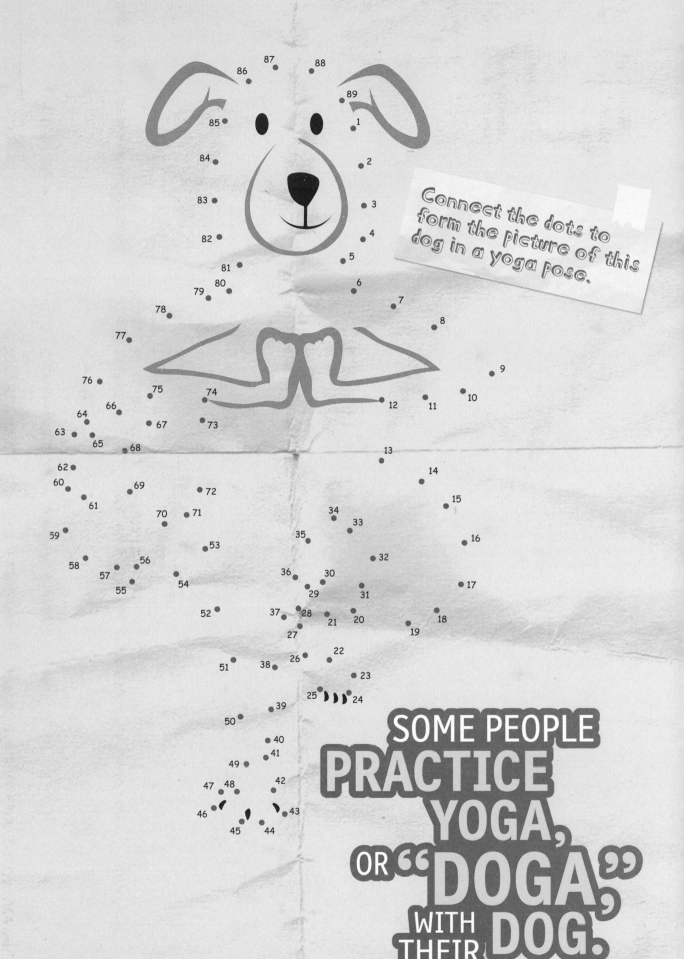

Connect the dots to form the picture of this dog in a yoga pose.

SOME PEOPLE PRACTICE YOGA, OR "DOGA," WITH THEIR DOG.

The world's **LARGEST MAZE**, the Dole Pineapple Garden Maze in Hawaii, U.S.A., has **2.5 MILES** (4 km) **OF PATHS** made with **MORE THAN 14,000 PLANTS.**

Can you make your way out of this fruity maze?

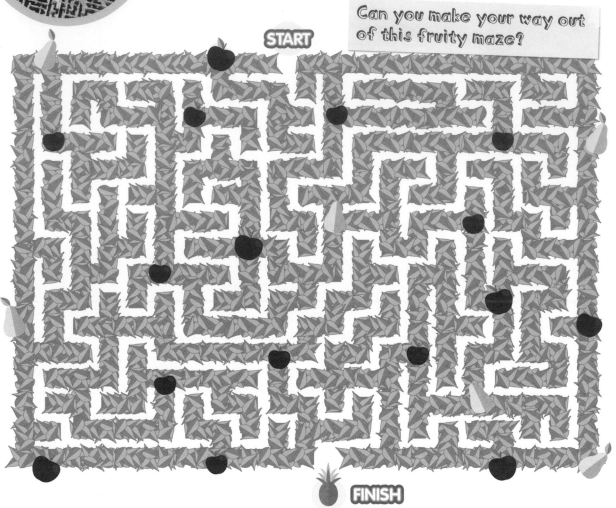

START

FINISH

An ancient Chinese soup recipe contains SIMMERED BIRD NESTS.

What's in your soup? Create a recipe, too.

You can buy a **CUPCAKE-SHAPED DESIGNER HANDBAG** with strawberry- and chocolate-colored crystals for **$4,295.**

Doesn't that make you hungry? Design your own food-themed bag. How about some matching shoes and a hat?

A **CUDDLY ROBOT** has been used in experiments to **CHEER UP LONELY PEOPLE.**

What would your robot say that would cheer you up?

Add some parts to this robot and then color it in.

25

Marine iguanas SNEEZE to get rid of EXTRA SALT in their bodies.

A squid can change its color and pattern in 700 milliseconds—almost in the blink of an eye.

Draw a pattern on one of these squids and color it. Then, blink—and draw a new pattern on the other squid!

There once was a hungry iguana
That proceeded to eat all the fauna.
It liked its food salty ...

Finish the poem! It doesn't have to rhyme.

A flawless
PINK DIAMOND
was auctioned for
$83 million.

Design a ring for each hand—or every finger! A matching watch would be nice, too.

This ONE-INCH-LONG CHAMELEON fits on the head of a matchstick.

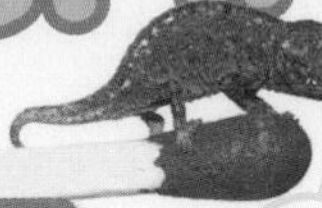

(2.5-cm)

ACTUAL SIZE

Color this scene and draw tiny chameleons where no one will find them!

A giraffe sleeps 90 minutes a day.

A giraffe sleepover would be fun. You could stay up all night and play Twister. What else would you do?

Flamingos apply "makeup" to appear more pink.

Color these flamingos pink, pinker, and pinkest! Or make them your favorite color.

The PUNCH of the mantis shrimp is as fast as a bullet.

This little shrimp's punch is not only fast but also super powerful. Which superpower would you like to possess? Draw a picture of yourself with an extraordinary power.

Male pufferfish use their **fins to draw** patterns in the sand.

This fish is trying so hard to impress the female fish. Help him write a love note to his future mate.

Women in 14th-century Europe wore **enormous** cone-shaped headdresses. Some were **so big,** architects had to **redesign doorways** so these women could fit through them!

Create some fashion-forward hats for you and your friends.

An ANCIENT MACHINE was discovered in 1900, but no one knows how it works.

What do you suppose this machine could do? **Finish building it.**

A blue whale's **largest veins** are so big, **you could swim** through them.

What a trip that would be! Design your swimsuit and pack the suitcase with your gear.

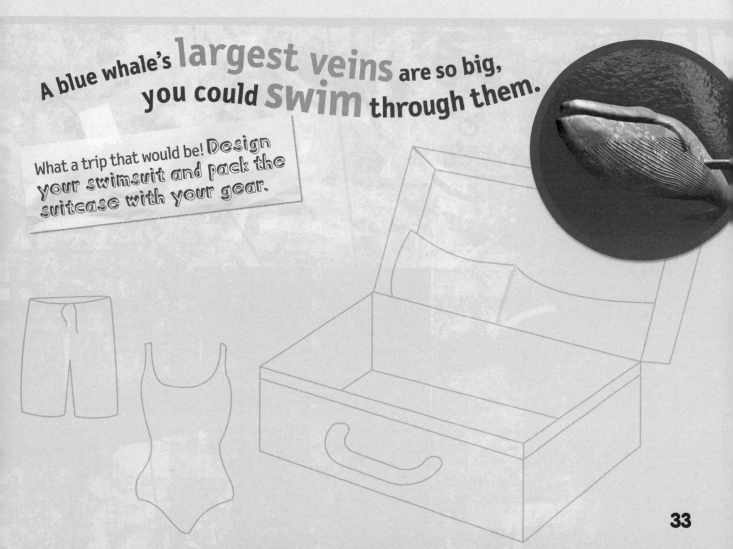

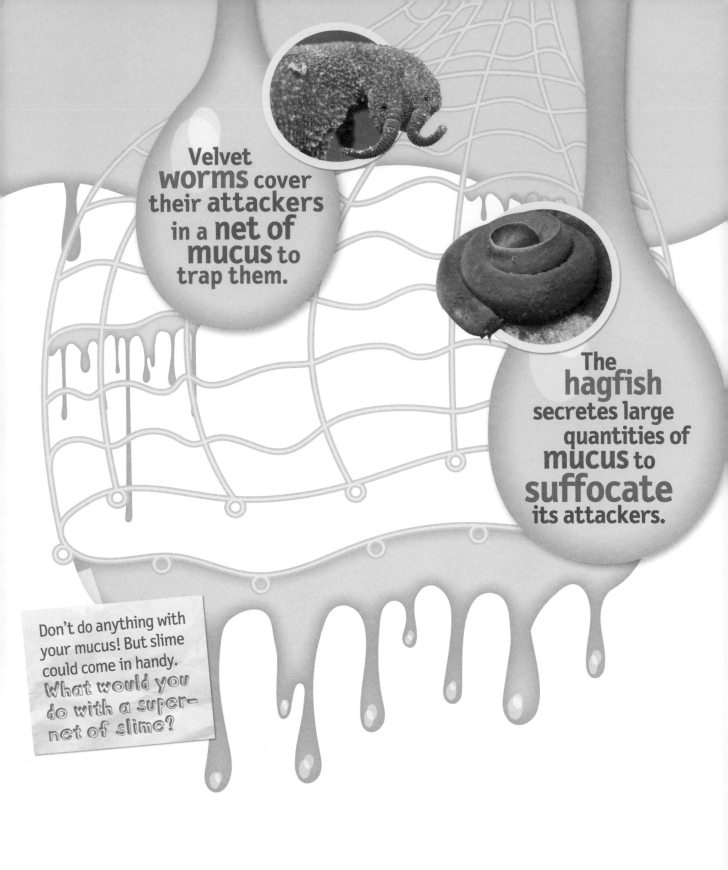

Velvet **worms** cover their **attackers** in a **net of mucus** to trap them.

The **hagfish** secretes large quantities of **mucus** to **suffocate** its attackers.

Don't do anything with your mucus! But slime could come in handy. *What would you do with a super-net of slime?*

PET FOOD companies hire people as TASTE TESTERS.

Not sure that's your dream job? Get a head start on your career with this quiz! Check your answers in the back.

1. What does a museologist do?

a. works in a museum
b. studies people who serve as muses, who inspire artists
c. works in the music industry

2. What does a fish and game warden do?

a. guards fish and animals that are imprisoned
b. organizes fishing, games, and other fun activities
c. inspects and protects fish and wildlife areas

3. What does a green marketer do?

a. advises companies on how to make the most money
b. markets green-colored products, especially clothing
c. markets products that are environmentally friendly

There are **119 grooves** on the edge of a U.S. quarter.

Design a coin featuring you! What else will appear on the money? Your house? Your best friend or pet?

The U.S. **silver dollar** has two nicknames: **Ferris wheel** and **cartwheel**.

Carrier shell snails
decorate themselves
with other **shells** and **scraps** like **bottle caps.**

These shells are so plain!
Help decorate them.

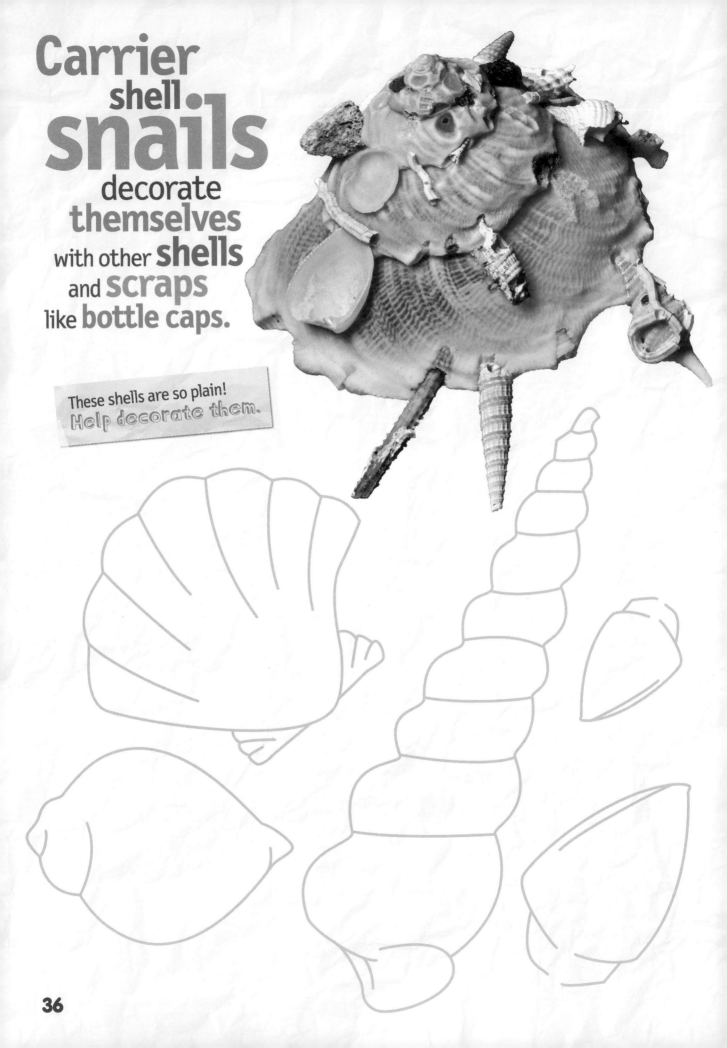

One **desert spider** escapes predators by **cartwheeling.**

Spider gymnastics! Imagine what spiders might do on this equipment.

Beetles discovered in Papua New Guinea are given names chosen at random from a phone book.

This beetle is named after you! What does it look like?

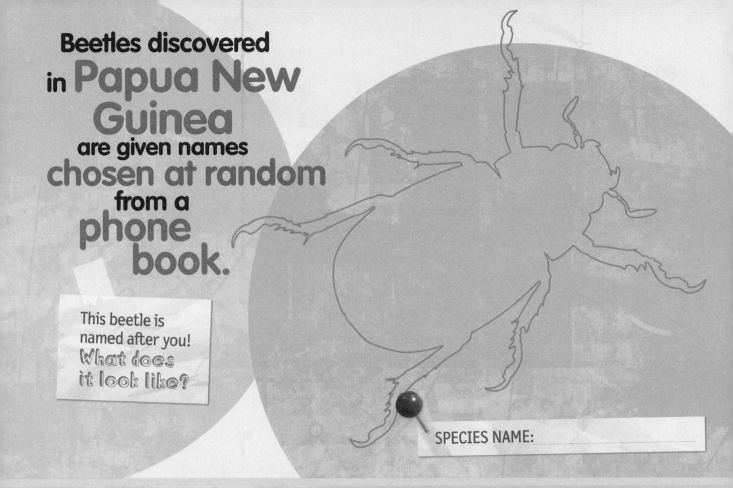

SPECIES NAME: _____

Draw and color some tiny pictures of these really big animals! Can you think of any others?

manatee
American alligator

hippopotamus
rhinoceros

shark
king cobra

One artist makes tiny sculptures from grains of rice.

Find the beetles hiding in this word search. Words may be found horizontally, vertically, and diagonally, forward or backward.

```
        G W A H
      C A R P E T
    P H E C S R A S
    D I T I J C O E
  G J X L I O U V F L
  D I V I N G L N A I
  R E Y W A S E T E D
  R B A R A C S R L X
  D U N G O T A T O P
  U E S E N A P A J M
  N T R E I D L O S O
  R U D N U O R G N L
```

CARPET   OIL
DIVING   OX
DUNG   POTATO
GROUND   SAWYER
HERCULES   SCARAB
JAPANESE   SILVER
JUNE   SOLDIER
LEAF   TIGER

Elephants can produce about 100 POUNDS (45 kg) of DUNG A DAY.

That's a lot of dung. Don't draw that—you'll wear out all your brown crayons! Instead, finish these drawings of beetles.

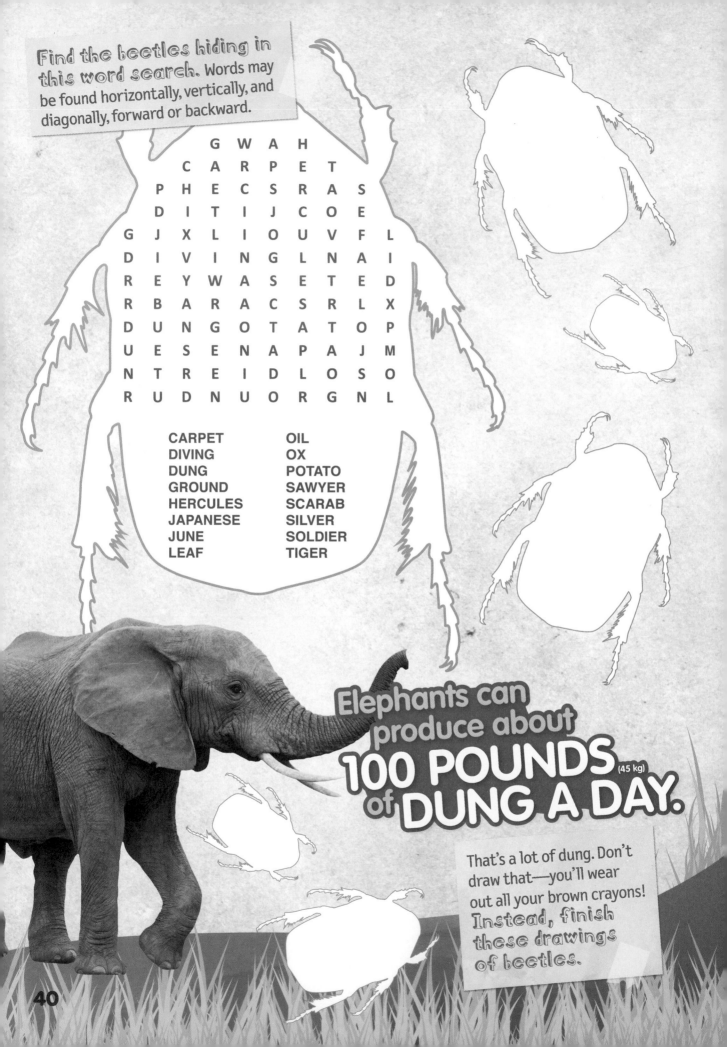

Adult beetles **SUCK THE LIQUID** from **DUNG FOR NUTRITION.**

FINISH

START

Dung beetles can bury **250 TIMES THEIR OWN WEIGHT** in dung in one day.

Help this beetle roll the dung up the hill!

Former U.S. president **Lyndon B. Johnson** **loved helicopters** so much that he had his **Oval Office chair** made from a real **helicopter seat.**

What would you bring to the Oval Office if you were president of the United States?

A "Code V" at a Disney park means a visitor has **thrown up.**

Too much cotton candy, pizza, and chips before riding the roller coaster? Sit awhile and find the ten differences between these two scenes.

Hundreds of years ago, **Russians built the first roller coasters from ice.**

In the early 1900s, **the Olympics** included contests in **art, literature,** and **music.**

During the 1928 Olympic **rowing race,** one competitor **stopped** to let a **family of ducks** pass— and **still won.**

```
W  A  S  O  C  C  E  R  H  S  I  N  N  E  T  E  L  B  A  T
I  C  E  H  O  C  K  E  Y  V  O  L  G  H  B  O  X  I  N  G
G  N  I  E  O  N  A  C  G  Y  M  N  A  S  T  I  C  S  N  E
N  R  Y  I  O  E  B  N  O  I  B  L  F  B  R  H  I  Y
   I  T  C  R  T  A  I  L  L  E  L  Y  U  J  L  R
   I  E  G  R  I  C  W  U  M  A  G  K  I  E
      K  I  Y  Y  N  Y  G  T  B  U  A  H
      S  C  U  E  G  E  Y  D  S  C
      G  T  E  F  O  L  H  N  R  O
      N  O  T  N  I  M  D  A  B  L
      I  G  N  I  W  O  R  H  O  L
      T  G  R  E  D  B  T  M  B  A
      A  N  N  U  B  A  E  G  S  B
      K  I  J  I  G  N  N  O  L  Y
      S  L  N  S  L  I  N  L  E  E
      D  R  I  H  M  T  I  F  D  L
      E  U  V  M  U  M  S  P  G  L
      E  C  I  C  R  T  T  E  H  O
      P  W  D  I  V  I  N  G  R  V
      S  O  L  O  P  R  E  T  A  W
```

ARCHERY
BADMINTON
BOBSLED
BOXING
CANOEING
CURLING
CYCLING
DIVING
FENCING
GOLF
GYMNASTICS
HANDBALL
ICE HOCKEY
JUDO

LUGE
ROWING
RUGBY
SAILING
SHOOTING
SKIING
SOCCER
SPEED SKATING
SWIMMING
TABLE TENNIS
TENNIS
VOLLEYBALL
WATER POLO
WRESTLING

You've just made the Olympic team! What sport would you like to play in the games? **See how many of these sports you can find in this word search.** Words may be found horizontally, vertically, and diagonally, forward or backward.

44

Would you prefer to draw something or write about sports? Use the empty space to do either!

It's time for the medals ceremony! What will your medal look like?

45

Chickens with white earlobes lay white eggs; chickens with red earlobes lay brown eggs.

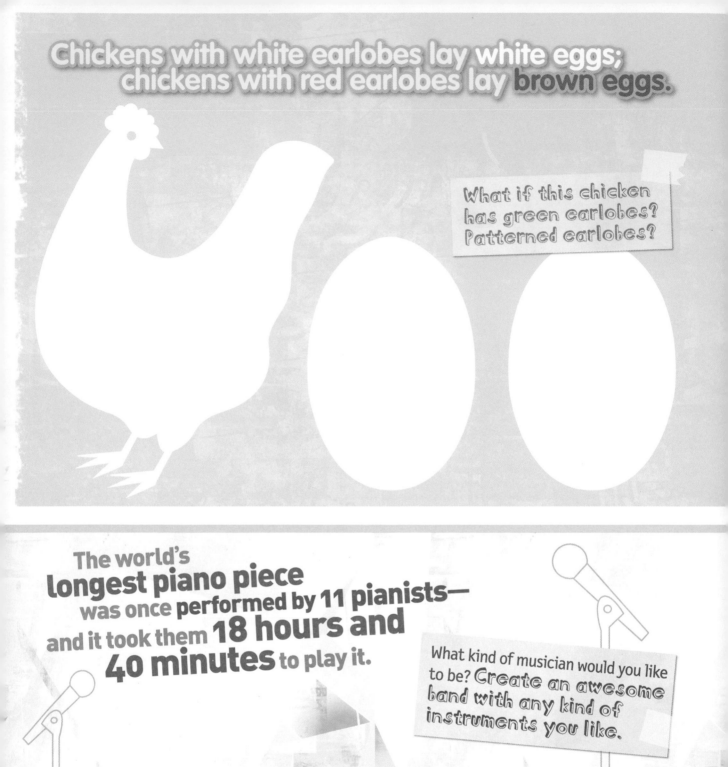

What if this chicken has green earlobes? Patterned earlobes?

The world's **longest piano piece** was once performed by **11 pianists**— and it took them **18 hours and 40 minutes** to play it.

What kind of musician would you like to be? Create an awesome band with any kind of instruments you like.

Doodling can help you concentrate.

brainstorm

crea

Focus! Start doodling!

draw

There's a bright red waterfall in Antarctica.

Microbes and other teeny tiny living things are responsible for turning the waterfall red. But don't let them scare you. Here, they're just words on a page! Draw some happy penguins slipping and sliding with these red words.

One species of GLASS FROG looks like Kermit the Frog.

A frog usually has long legs and smooth skin that is covered in mucus. A toad usually has shorter legs and rough skin. Draw and color one of each!

The Suriname SEA TOAD'S BABIES are born through the SKIN on their mother's back.

Name your racehorse! Which horse will win? Come up with as many names as you like and write them on the scoreboard. Draw your horses on the track.

1
2
3
4
5

1
2
3
4
5

A racehorse's official name can be no longer than 18 characters.

At a **spa in Japan,** you can soak in a tub of **tea** or **coffee.**

THE MARS ROVER CURIOSITY CAN TAKE A SELFIE.

Imagine yourself on Mars!
Place yourself in this picture with Curiosity.

You can write about 45,000 words with an average pencil.

You can start here! Complete this crossword puzzle made up of words related to—what else?—words!

Across

2 Describes a verb or adjective

5 Last three letters of a story?

6 A book that lists words and their meanings

8 A story in a newspaper

9 Short messages, often on small pieces of paper

12 A message sent electronically

14 A piece of writing that may use 4 Down

16 A type of airplane that you can write on

18 English and math are each a ___ in school

20 Removes a pencil's mistakes

21 Quick way to write something down

22 "Repeat" another's words

Down

1 A note that might be on a board

3 An educational place for a worm?

4 "Time," "lime," and "grime" are words that ___

7 A book of synonyms

10 What has a beginning, a middle, and an end?

11 A soup with letters

13 A, B, or C

15 Secret messages that need to be deciphered

16 Group of words that isn't a full sentence

17 This special bird carried secret messages for soldiers in World War I

19 Written words in a book

The giant pitcher plant can catch **mice** and **rats** and eat them.

The largest **dinosaurs** were vegetarians.

No rodents at this table! So, what's for lunch? Don't forget to draw something for a very hungry dinosaur—just in case one shows up.

There are
190-million-year-old
dinosaur footprints near **Moab, Utah,** U.S.A.

FINISH

This dino mom needs to get back to her nest! Help her find the right path to it.

START

A mouthful of seawater may hold tens of thousands of ZOOPLANKTON.

Gulp! What if they all decided to spend the day on the beach? Don't forget the sunscreen!

An Australian man **filled three jars** with his **belly button lint** that he collected **over 26 years.**

What would you fill these containers with? Start a collection!

Scientists once collected **24,999 toenail clippings** for a study.

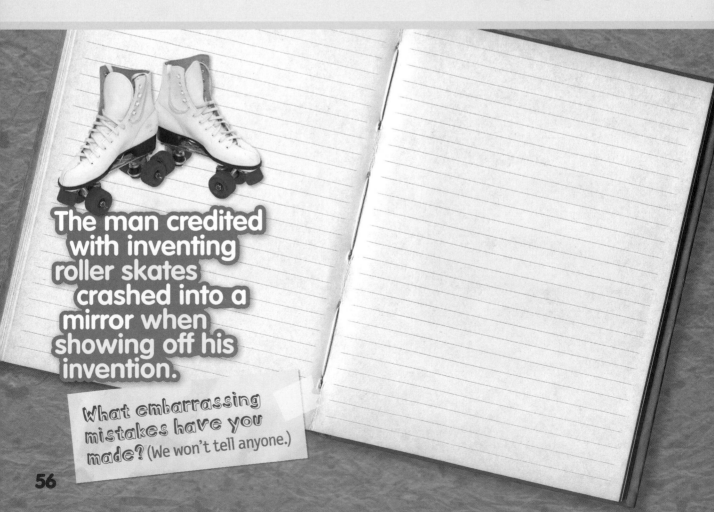

The man credited with inventing roller skates crashed into a mirror when showing off his invention.

What embarrassing mistakes have you made? (We won't tell anyone.)

NASA's Hubble telescope captured an image of a **galaxy cluster** that looks like a **smiley face.**

Connect these dots to form the constellation Leo.

Bonus Activity!
Grab an adult and go to *spaceplace.nasa.gov/voyager-to-stars/en.*
See if you can guess the sounds on the recordings carried aboard the Voyagers 1 and 2 spacecraft as they explore our star system and beyond. What message would you send to aliens who might live outside our solar system?

The U.S. Navy built a robot that swims and looks like a shark.

Your mission: Protect these coral reefs from intruders! Show us your ideas.

There are more than **40,000 lightbulbs** in **Buckingham Palace.**

It would be fun to live in a castle. What would yours look like? Finish the drawing, then decorate your new castle.

The **world's biggest** inhabited **palace** has **1,788 rooms.**

22,000 people and **6,000 horses** lived with the King of France at his **Versailles palace.**

Chihuahua + **dachshund** = **chiweenie**

Why adopt a cool mutt?

Create your own mixtures by combining these breeds. Then write an ad for a rescue league describing how cool mutts are and why they should be adopted! Don't forget to draw pictures of the new breeds!

poodle	bloodhound	Newfoundland
bulldog	borzoi	Pekingese
Labrador	boxer	whippet
basenji	collie	sheltie
beagle	Dalmatian	

A **405-year-old clam** found in 2007 was alive when **Shakespeare** was writing *Macbeth.*

Perhaps the clam inspired some of Shakespeare's quotations! Have some fun with these famous quotations from the Bard by asking a friend to **fill in the blanks with the parts of speech that are shown.** Then read the sayings aloud. The actual quotations can be found on page 154.

To _____ (VERB), or not to _____ (SAME VERB): That is the question.

Double, double _____ (NOUN) and trouble; _____ (NOUN) burn, and _____ (NOUN) bubble.

There's _____ (NOUN, PLURAL) in men's smiles.

_____ (NOUN, PLURAL), Romans, countrymen, lend me your _____ (NOUN, PLURAL).

_____ (EXCLAMATION), good night! _____ (NOUN) is such _____ (ADJECTIVE) _____ (NOUN), that I shall say _____ (SAME EXCLAMATION) till it be morrow.

Studies show that the average daydream is about 14 seconds long.

What are you daydreaming about today?

In India, kids throw a **lost tooth** onto **the roof** and ask that **a sparrow** bring a new one.

In some countries, a **mouse** or a **rabbit**, **not a fairy**, brings money to children for lost teeth.

What if all those teeth ended up in one place? What would the people there do with them?

In some Middle Eastern countries, **children throw** a **lost tooth** toward the **sun.**

Welcome to the LAND OF LOST TEETH

A baby rabbit is called a kitten.

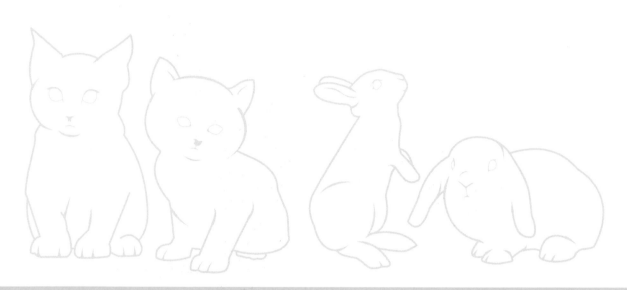

Color these kittens! Then color the other kittens! Then draw some more—these bunnies and cats are very social.

Some ORCHIDS smell like DEAD MICE.

Follow your nose and find the strong-smelling things in this word search. Words may be found horizontally, vertically, and diagonally, forward or backward.

BAD BREATH	FEET	PERFUME	TRASH
BODY ODOR	FISH	SKUNK	VOMIT
CHEESE	GARLIC	SOUR MILK	
COFFEE	MOLD	SWEAT	
EGG	ONIONS	TAR	

```
        T               T
T R B O D Y O D O R   R
A T E E F F O C K   K
S W E R T M O L D   D
H J G A R L I C A   A
R D G T I M O V C   C
B A D B R E A T H   H
O E M U F R E P E   E
S N O I N O N O E   E
H S I F T A E W S   S
W E K N U K S P E   E
```

Some tribes on New Guinea use **bird of paradise feathers** as **money.**

Ruffle some feathers! Give these birds some extreme plumage!

Many birds' **feathers weigh more** than their **bones.**

NASA is developing a 3-D printer that it hopes will "print" edible pizzas.

"National School Bus Glossy Yellow" is the actual name of the **paint color** used on **school buses** in the United States and Canada.

This school bus wants to get noticed! What should it look like? Finish drawing the bus, then color it.

People with **TETRACHROMACY** can see about **100 MILLION colors**— the average person can see only **about 1 MILLION.**

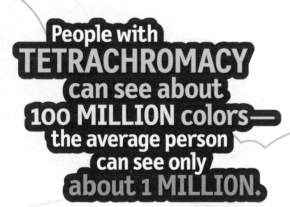

They're going to need a bigger crayon box! Finish the scene using as many colors as you can find.

Before every **major league** game, **umpires** rub each baseball **with mud.**

You're the ump in this scene. Show us what's happening here.

Astronaut Neil Armstrong left his **boots** on the **moon**.

EARTHLING SOUVENIRS

What would you leave on the moon?

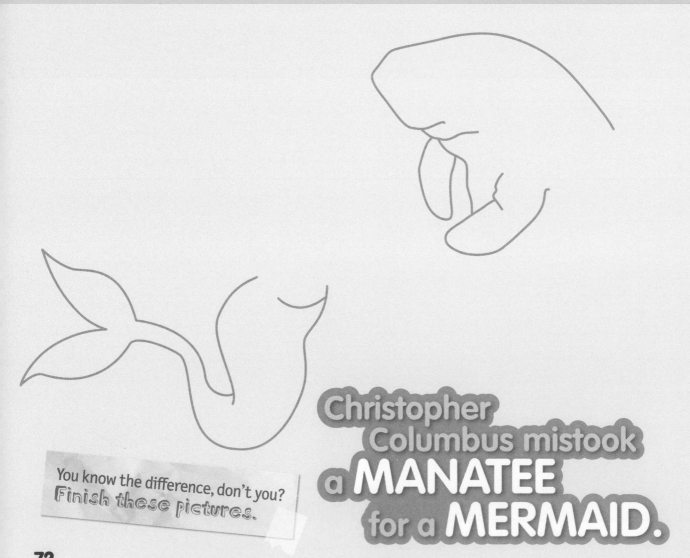

You know the difference, don't you? Finish these pictures.

Christopher Columbus mistook a **MANATEE** for a **MERMAID**.

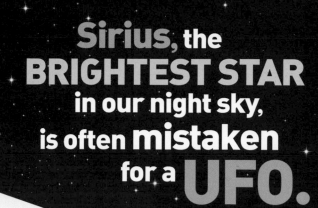

Sirius, the **BRIGHTEST STAR** in our night sky, is often **mistaken** for a **UFO.**

TOP SECRET

INTERNATIONAL

FILE NO

Your name:

Location of sighting:

Date and time of day:

Number of objects:

Witnesses:

DID THE OBJECT ...

- move?
- change shape?
- change color?
- change brightness?
- emit smoke?
- leave a trail?
- drop anything?

Write a report to the International UFO Bureau about an alien spacecraft you might have seen. Draw a detailed picture of the UFO.

African lions catch about 25 percent of the prey they chase.

```
      L   S   S   W   A   J
T     T   T   E   M   R   E           T
C     E   N   A   L   I   E   C   N   N
H     S   U   R   C   M   T   L   O   O
A     F   H   T   A   I   E   A   L   S
R     K   L   L   T   C   D   W   A   I
G     C   I   E   N   E   R   S   T   O
E     I   D   A   E   D   Y   A   L   P
C     K   I   P   T   T   H   G   I   F
Y     S   L   L   I   U   Q       C
```

Word prey! Hunt for these words related to predators and prey. Don't let anyone sneak up and surprise you while you're working! Words may be found horizontally, vertically, and diagonally, forward or backward.

CHARGE	HUNT	QUILLS
CLAWS	JAWS	SMELL
CRUSH	KICK	SPEED
DETER	MIMIC	STARTLE
FIGHT	PLAY DEAD	TALON
FLEE	POISON	TENTACLES

Bonus Activity!
After you circle all of the words, unscramble the unused letters to discover the shocking way that some animals attack their prey.

__ __ __ __ __ __ __ __ __ __ __ __ __ __ __ __ __ __ __

To stop a predator, Japanese **honeybees** **vibrate** until their **hive gets** so **hot**, the **intruder dies.**

Some **sea cucumbers** **confuse** their **enemies** by ejecting their own **organs** out of **their rear end.**

Tia the **Neapolitan mastiff** gave birth to **24 puppies** in one litter.

That's a lot of puppies! Finish drawing these pups, and then color them.

In the **Middle Ages,** people put **thyme sprigs** under their pillows to **stop nightmares.**

Have you had any weird dreams lately? Draw or describe your dreams here.

A study found that the **longer** you **sleep,** the **stranger** your **dreams** become.

Barbie has had more than 150 jobs and has run for president six times.

These dolls are explorers! One is headed out on a deep-sea expedition; the other is on her way to an archaeological dig in the Sahara. What kind of gear will they need for their adventures?

CATS COMMUNICATE using at least 16 known "CAT WORDS."

What are these cats saying?

Dogs can make about 100 different facial expressions.

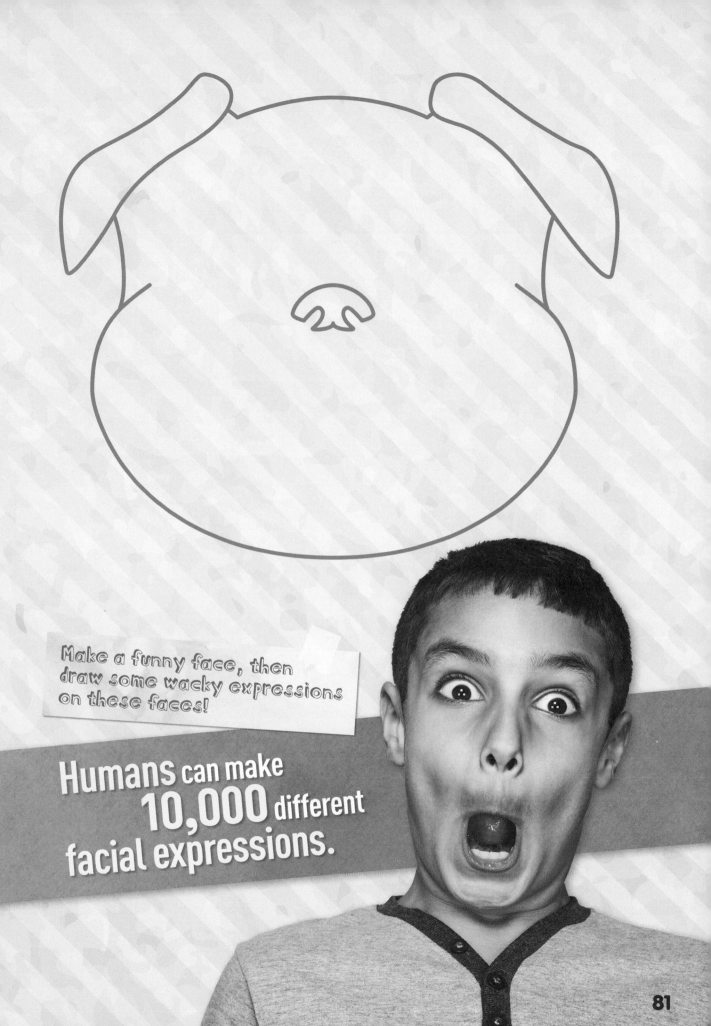

Make a funny face, then draw some wacky expressions on these faces!

Humans can make **10,000** different facial expressions.

What do you think? Draw and color these dinos!

No one knows what color dinosaurs were.

A Taiwanese airline flies HELLO KITTY–THEMED JETS.

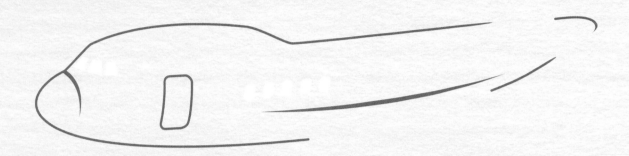

Your new airline is about to take off. **Design an awesome new plane.** The sky's the limit, so make it interesting!

U.S. president Theodore Roosevelt had a pet hyena.

Hmmm, a pet hyena? What would you name him or her? In the meantime, **finish this poem—it doesn't have to rhyme!**

There was a courageous hyena;

She went by the name of Edwina.

She never did laugh …

You can buy a **$25,000 doghouse** that comes with **air-conditioning** and a **music system.**

This dog wants a better doghouse!
Can you help?

There's an annual **beauty pageant for camels** in the United Arab Emirates, a country in Asia.

What do you think the camels wear for the competition?

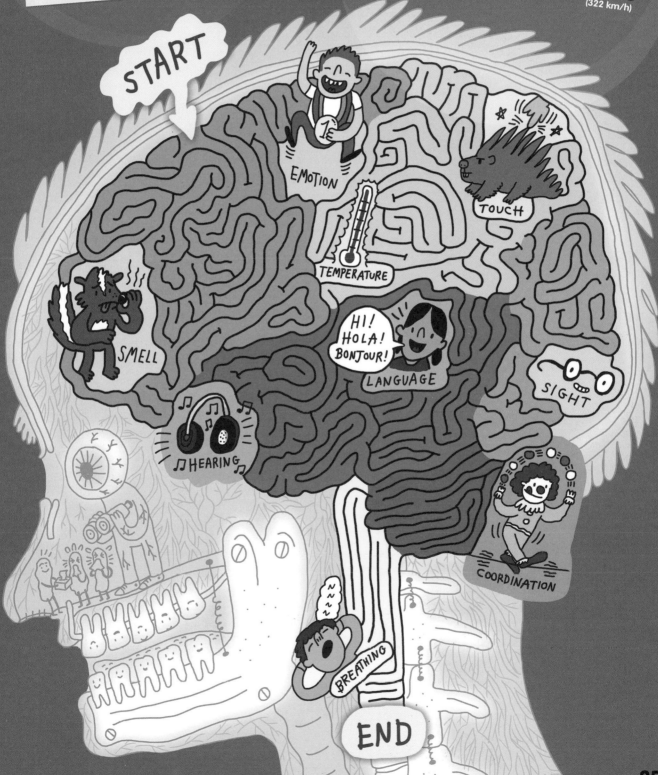

A **sculpture** outside the **headquarters** of the **CIA,** a **U.S. spy agency, contains four different secret codes.**

Use the key to decode these messages, and then use the code to create your own secret messages.

KEY

The U.S. Secret Service uses code names for important people. One former vice president's daughter's code name was Smurfette.

During the **American Revolution,** one spy used the **laundry** on her **clothesline** to signal to other spies.

A silkworm uses about a HALF MILE (0.8 km) of SPIT to build its COCOON.

Help this silkworm make its way to the mulberry leaf.

START

FINISH

The offspring of a whale and a dolphin is a wholphin.

Squirtle

A GEEP is part goat, part sheep.

Make your own mash-up!
Create new animals by mixing up these names, then draw and color what your new creature would look like.

hippo	tree frog	chameleon	manatee
elephant	squirrel	otter	lizard
monkey	turtle	crocodile	rattlesnake
giant panda	penguin	ant	shark
polar bear	beaver	elk	flounder

In a **student experiment** on the International Space Station, the **jumping spider** Nefertiti was able to **"pounce"** and **catch flies** even in **zero gravity.**

You can propose an idea for an experiment in space! What experiment would you like NASA to conduct? What supplies would they need? What question would you like NASA to answer?

One **space shuttle** blasted off with about 2,500 baby jellyfish on board.

A sculptor carved chairs, a table, and a sofa out of chocolate.

ALL

Who would you invite to your chocolate dinner party?

Some three million SUNKEN SHIPS lie on the ocean floor.

Let's go on a treasure hunt! Find the ten hidden treasures on this ship.

A Spanish scientist invented **ICE CREAM** that **CHANGES COLORS** when licked.

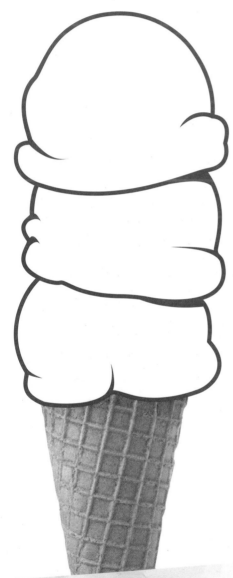

What color are these ice-cream flavors? Don't forget the toppings!

What's coming out of this vending machine? You don't need any money!

FREE!

Special **vending machines** in Istanbul, Turkey, automatically dispense **food** and **water** for **dogs.**

There are **more than** 20,000 TV **stations** in the world.

What's playing on these TVs?

Macaroni and **cheese**, **asparagus**, and **cotton candy** are not only foods; they're also **crayon colors.**

Color these crayons and give them each a funny name.

A famous painting

was once accidentally **hung upside down** and **left on display** for **46 days** in a New York City **museum.**

Complete these drawings, matching top and bottom or left and right.

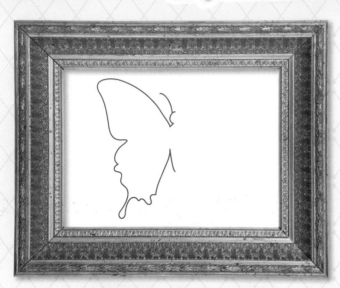

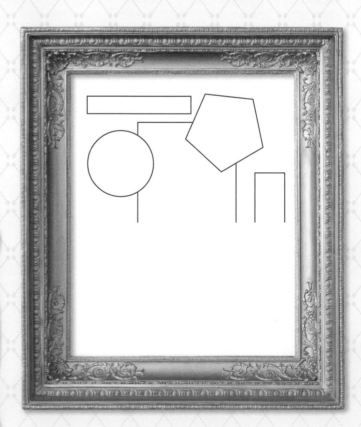

Extreme surfers ride the Amazon River's *pororoca,* A MASSIVE WAVE as tall as **12 feet** (4 m) —some daredevils surf for more than **7 miles.** (11 km)

Surf's up! This pink river dolphin wants you to join in the fun. What are you riding? Draw your board.

Every year, more than **EIGHT BILLION**
Sweethearts candy conversation hearts
are made—enough love to **GIVE ONE** to
every person in the **world.**

COOL

SURE LOVE

LOVE NOTE

U-R CUTE

CUP CAKE

NICE BOY

BE MINE

COOL DUDE

HEY DUDE

MAD4 YOU

I'M REAL

Think of some
new sayings—
sweet or funny
or both—for
these candies
and valentines.

Fried scorpions on skewers are a popular snack in Beijing, China.

It's movie time! Turn the lights down and set out some popcorn, crackers, and cheese! Fill these bowls with some wacky snacks.

Casu marzu, cheese infested with live, wriggling maggots, is considered a delicacy in Italy.

Sometimes animals hitch a ride across the ocean to a new continent.

Show this iguana how to get from South America to the Galápagos Islands.

GALÁPAGOS ISLANDS

START

FINISH

SOUTH AMERICA

SOUTH AMERICA

The cherimoya fruit, native to South America, tastes like bubblegum.

That's just a few of the many awesome plant and animal species of South America. See how fast you can unscramble the names of some others.

Kinkajous can twist their hind feet backwards to climb trees.

PAYARBCA

_____

ETER OFRG

_____

LOMRAALID

_____

TERNATEA

_____

MALAL

_____

PITAR

_____

DOCHIR

_____

EPSDETCALC RBEA

_____

OSMS

_____

CAICAA

_____

VEMGANOR

_____

The WORLD'S LARGEST GINGERBREAD VILLAGE required 3,550 POUNDS OF ICING, (1,610 kg) 700 POUNDS OF CANDY, and (318 kg) 600 POUNDS OF DOUGH. (272 kg)

You're the village architect! Design your village, then decorate it using whatever you like.

Alpaca moms

hum to comfort their babies.

Finish this lullaby—quick, before you fall asleep!

Lil' alpaca, go to sleep,

Close your eyes, don't make a peep.

Thousands of glowworms look like a starry sky in one New Zealand cave.

Write a postcard from someplace weird!

WISH YOU WERE HERE IN

Sandstone formations in one Utah, U.S.A., park look like goblins.

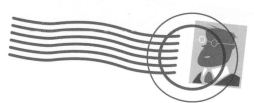

TO:

The sailing stones at Racetrack Playa in Death Valley, U.S.A., are huge rocks that "sail" across the ground.

LENTICULAR CLOUDS, which are hat-shaped, are often MISTAKEN for UFOs.

Find these cloud words in this word search. Words may be found horizontally, vertically, and diagonally, forward or backward.

```
              G R A L I G H T N I N G
    W I N D S P E E D S U T A M M A M
    N R E T T A P D U O L C E V E R
  N U I A L E N S S H A P E D A I L F
  I H A I E D F A T I N O F O R M R O
  M T T R N D L L E C R E P U S A F G
  B N S F N I O F L E N T I C U L A R A
G O E I L U E A P I L E U S C L O U D
N S C O O F S T A L T O S T R A T U S
I T U M W J E T S T R E A M C I R R U S
R R L E V A W Y T I V A R G O I N C U S
M A I C S W Y F R E C U A S G N I Y L F
A T T O R N A D I C E C R Y S T A L S
E U C E E R I V T G U L A C I T R E V
T S O F D O S R E M R V O N K A R M A N
S U N P A N R U U C O A V E L U M
    U T R A Y L C R L A Y E R E D
    R E D N U H T R M O L O F
      T S H E L F A B U T D
        X                 D
```

AIR FLOW	FUNNEL	MAMMATUS	TORNADIC
ALTOSTRATUS	GRAVITY WAVE	MOIST AIR	UPDRAFT
ARCUS	GRAY	NIMBOSTRATUS	VELUM
ATINOFORM	ICE CRYSTALS	NOCTILUCENT	VERTICAL
CLOUD PATTERN	INCUS	PILEUS CLOUD	VIRGA
CUMULUS	JETSTREAM CIRRUS	RAIN	VORTEX
EDDIES	LAYERED	SHELF	WAVE CLOUD
FLOAT	LENS SHAPED	STEAM RING	WINDSPEED
FLYING SAUCER	LENTICULAR	SUPERCELL	
FOG	LIGHTNING	THUNDER	

Sesame Street's Oscar the Grouch was originally orange.

Draw some weird and wacky puppets of your own!

The SUN sets in the EAST on VENUS.

Sunsets on MARS are BLUE.

My Shot

Imagine the wackiest sunset ever—then draw it here!

There's a **town**
in Oregon, U.S.A., named

Boring.

Ho-hum. Come up with a
new, interesting name
for the town and design
its welcome sign.

What **toys** would you bring with you on a trip to the International Space Station? Choose one you have and create a new one, if you like.

A **Buzz Lightyear** action figure spent 15 months on the International Space Station.

A Japanese artist makes shells for HERMIT CRABS that look like CITY SKYLINES.

These hermit crabs decided to move to the city! **What will their neighborhood look like?**

Bonus Activity!

Like weird-looking marine species? Like to mix and match? Grab an adult and go to *games.noaa.gov/mix_match*. You'll discover species that share their habitat with hermit crabs in and around the Chesapeake Bay, U.S.A.

Invent a toy or game!
Be sure to include the rules, if any.
And think of a good name.

The FRISBEE was originally named the Pluto Platter.

Baby **seahorses eat** about **3,000 pieces** of **food** a day.

Seahorses can move their eyes in two directions at once.

These baby seahorses are hungry! But each one is missing something. Complete the drawings and color them in so they can hunt for food.

Seahorse fathers carry eggs in a **pouch** and **give birth** to their babies.

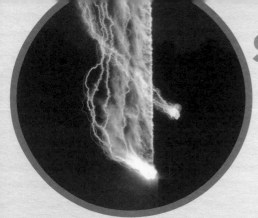

Scientists recently made a picture of thunder.

Draw a picture of an awesome storm. Don't forget the thunder snow!

Competitors race **tricked-out portable potties** at the **annual outhouse races** in Nevada, U.S.A.

Construct the winning-est portable potty for the race.

During World War II,

Navajo Indian soldiers developed an

unbreakable secret code

for the U.S. military.

Decode this message, then create your own using the Navajo code dictionary shown below.

TSE-GAH DZEH DIBEH-YAZZIE DIBEH-YAZZIE NE-AHS-JAH!

ALPHABET	NAVAJO WORD	ALPHABET	NAVAJO WORD
A	WOL-LA-CHEE	N	TSAH
B	NA-HASH-CHID	O	NE-AHS-JAH
C	MOASI	P	CLA-GI-AIH
D	LHA-CHA-EH	Q	CA-YEILTH
E	DZEH	R	GAH
F	TSA-E-DONIN-EE	S	DIBEH
G	AH-TAD	T	D-AH
H	TSE-GAH	U	SHI-DA
I	TKIN	V	A-KEH-DI-GLINI
J	TKELE-CHO-G	W	GLOE-IH
K	JAD-HO-LONI	X	AL-NA-AS-DZOH
L	DIBEH-YAZZIE	Y	TSAH-AS-ZIH
M	TSIN-TLITI	Z	BESH-DO-TLIZ

The world's
**most expensive
baseball card**
—a 1909 Honus Wagner—
sold for **$2.8 million**
in 2007.

WAGNER, PITTSBURG

Draw a new trading
card. Who is on it?
Don't throw it out—it might
be worth millions someday!

Americans spend up
to **$40 million** on
baseball cards
each year.

It's illegal to sell a **haunted house** in New York, U.S.A., **without telling** the buyer.

Boo! Is this house haunted? Count the ghosts lurking in its nooks and crannies.

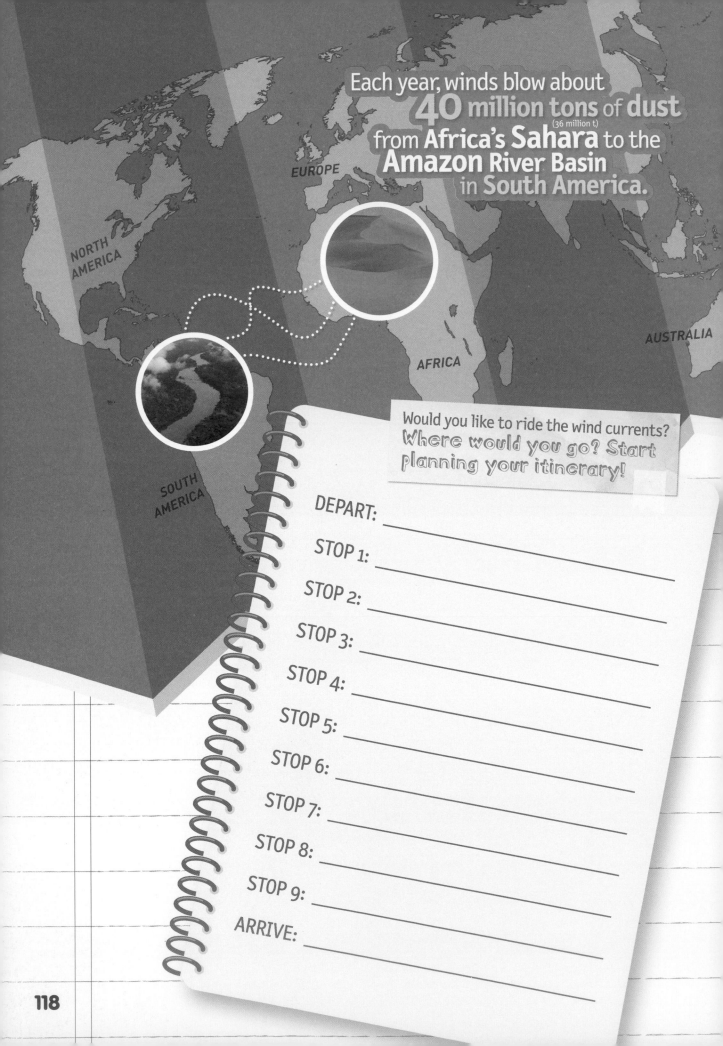

Each year, winds blow about **40 million tons** of **dust** (36 million t) from **Africa's Sahara** to the **Amazon River Basin** in **South America.**

NORTH AMERICA

EUROPE

AFRICA

AUSTRALIA

SOUTH AMERICA

Would you like to ride the wind currents? Where would you go? Start planning your itinerary!

DEPART: _____

STOP 1: _____

STOP 2: _____

STOP 3: _____

STOP 4: _____

STOP 5: _____

STOP 6: _____

STOP 7: _____

STOP 8: _____

STOP 9: _____

ARRIVE: _____

Some PREHISTORIC PEOPLE used MAMMOTH BONES to build their HOMES.

That probably scared off the big, bad wolf! Design your house using far-out materials.

119

French daredevil Eric Barone RODE A BIKE DOWN THE SIDE OF A VOLCANO at a record-setting 107 MILES AN HOUR.

(172 km/h)

The volcano was not erupting at the time, but his ride was still extreme! Where do you like to ride your bike? *Where else would you like to ride?*

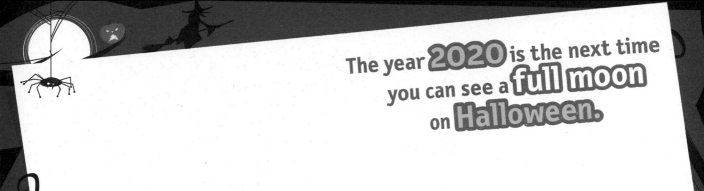

The year **2020** is the next time you can see a **full moon** on **Halloween.**

That gives you plenty of time to come up with an awesome costume! You can start planning right here.

People in **CHINA** have been eating pasta for **7,000 YEARS.**

That's a lot of pasta! How much do you think you've eaten? What do you like on your pasta?

The planet **Uranus** was almost named **George.**

The dwarf planet **Haumea** is nicknamed **Santa.**

Do you have a nickname? Do you know why you were given your name? Write your information on the name tag, and then decorate the tag.

Four asteroids are named after the Beatles.

The longest someone has ever held their breath is 22 minutes.

Find your way through this underwater maze in less than 22 minutes!

START

FINISH

A VOLCANIC ERUPTION in 1883 made the SUN look GREEN.

Color this sun green—or whatever color you like! What color are the trees—yellow? Is the sky blue—or orange? Color "outside the crayon box"!

BEES can be GREEN, BLUE, or RED.

A **RAINBOW** LOOKS DIFFERENT to EVERYONE who sees it.

There's a **PINK LAKE** in AUSTRALIA.

A man-made group of islands in Dubai, United Arab Emirates, is shaped like a world map.

If you had billions of dollars to spend on building islands, what would yours look like?

Tsar Peter the Great of Russia put a **special tax** on men who wore **beards.**

Beards have had a storied hairstory! Draw some interesting facial hair on these faces.

Hatshepsut, the only **female pharaoh** of Egypt, wore a **fake beard.**

Living in space is very different from living on Earth! Get ready for your trip to space by completing this crossword puzzle. Fit all the words into the white spaces in this grid.

3 letter words
Ice
Sun

4 letter words
Dark
Dawn
Moon
Star

5 letter words
Comet
Earth
Orbit
Tides
Venus

6 letter words
Planet
Pulsar
Quasar
Saturn

7 letter words
Gravity
Shuttle

9 letter words
Astronaut
Astronomy
Mars rover
Radiation
Supernova

It's impossible to whistle on the moon.

Flowers smell different in space.

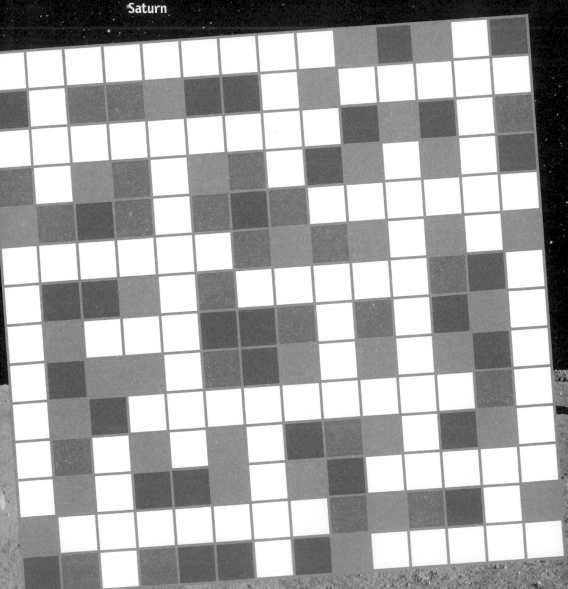

The
LARGEST BEATBOX
performance
involved more
than **4,500**
people.

The world record for
LONGEST DRUMROLL
is **8 hours, 1 minute,**
and **17 seconds.**

A group of pugs is called a grumble.

Can you match these other animal group names with the correct animals?

CLOUD Ⓐ
PARLIAMENT OR STARE Ⓑ
CUPBOARD Ⓒ
LOVELINESS Ⓓ
CACKLE Ⓔ
PRICKLE Ⓕ
ARMY OR COLONY OR FORGERY Ⓖ
STREAK OR AMBUSH Ⓗ
ZEAL Ⓘ
LEAP Ⓙ
FLAMBOYANCE OR STAND Ⓚ
SCURRY OR DRAY Ⓛ
RAFT Ⓜ
FLIGHT Ⓝ
TROOPS Ⓞ
LOUNGE Ⓟ
BASK OR FLOAT Ⓠ
TOWER Ⓡ
CRASH Ⓢ
FLOCK Ⓣ
CELEBRATION Ⓤ
COALITION Ⓥ
MOB OR COURT OR TROOP Ⓦ
BLOAT Ⓧ
COMPANY OR PANDEMONIUM Ⓨ
CARAVAN OR TRAIN Ⓩ

1 POLAR BEARS
2 SEA OTTERS
3 ZEBRAS
4 MONARCH BUTTERFLIES
5 HYENAS
6 MONKEYS
7 MACAWS
8 GIRAFFES
9 RHINOS
10 SQUIRRELS
11 CAMELS
12 CROCS
13 FLAMINGOS
14 FROGS
15 TIGERS
16 GRASSHOPPERS
17 HIPPOS
18 KANGAROOS
19 LADYBUGS
20 LEOPARDS
21 LIZARDS
22 OWLS
23 PANDAS
24 PARROTS
25 CHEETAHS
26 PORCUPINES

MY ANSWERS

A. _____   H. _____   O. _____   V. _____
B. _____   I. _____   P. _____   W. _____
C. _____   J. _____   Q. _____   X. _____
D. _____   K. _____   R. _____   Y. _____
E. _____   L. _____   S. _____   Z. _____
F. _____   M. _____   T. _____
G. _____   N. _____   U. _____

You drink the same **WATER** as the **dinosaurs, woolly mammoths,** the first humans, and **King Tut.**

This famous crowd is gathering at the water fountain! *Who else should come?*

One BMW car model was fitted with a "FLAMETHROWER" that could blast fire from below the doors.

Believe it or not, this model, which is supposed to deter car theft, is still legal in some places! Draw your dream car. Better add some high-tech defense mechanisms ... just in case.

In **ancient Rome,** the traditional **birthday food** was **porridge.**

Victorian parents used their **children's** birthday parties to **teach them manners.**

You probably have some different ideas for your celebration— start planning!

A **pig** was once tried for **murder.**

Help these critters get out of jail!

JAIL

A **pigeon** was arrested and charged with **spying.**

START

FINISH

137

Imagine what else these industrious crows and wasps could build if they worked together!

Some **WASPS** use **pebbles** as **HAMMERS** to build their **nests.**

New Caledonian **CROWS** make **right-handed** and **left-handed TOOLS.**

One artist uses **thousands** of colorful **jelly beans** to create colorful **"paintings."**

Create incredible inedible candy art.

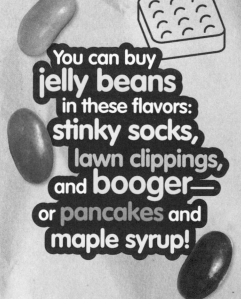

You can buy **jelly beans** in these flavors: **stinky socks,** lawn clippings, and **booger**— or pancakes and **maple syrup!**

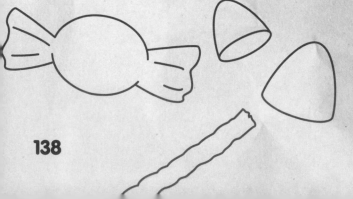

Sixteen-year-old **Lady Jane Grey** was the **queen of England** for **nine days.**

That's not a lot of time—you'd better get busy! What would you do if you were the leader of your country for nine days? *Make a list and present your top idea here.*

One parasite **makes its own** pine-and-lemon-scented **"perfume"** to attract a **mosquito host.**

That's weird—and kind of gross! Find the names of these parasites that have burrowed into the word search below. You might start to feel a little itchy. Words may be found horizontally, vertically, and diagonally, forward or backward.

G	U	I	N	E	A	W	O	R	M	
S	M	B	S	M	W	K	W	R	R	
C	R	O	R	U	C	M	O	A	O	
R	O	T	B	I	G	W	H	E	W	
E	W	F	T	M	P	N	C	L	N	
W	E	L	M	I	R	I	U	F	I	
W	P	Y	H	T	L	O	R	F	P	
O	A	W	B	E	D	B	U	G	O	
R	T	M	R	O	W	R	I	A	H	
M	R	O	W	T	A	L	F	W	M	

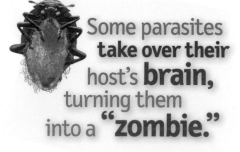

Some parasites **take over their** host's **brain,** turning them into a **"zombie."**

BED BUG
BOT FLY
FLATWORM
FLEA
FUNGUS
GUINEA WORM
HAIRWORM

LICE
MITE
PINWORM
SCREWWORM
TAPEWORM
TICK
WHIPWORM

An 18th-century man became famous for **walking** around England with **rocks piled** on his **head.**

That could give you a headache!
Draw a picture of why you'll be famous—or simply proud of yourself.

Up to
3,000 silkworm cocoons are
needed to produce
one pound (0.5 kg)
of silk.

Do you ever feel like crawling into a nice comfy cocoon? What would you make yours from?
Draw your cocoon!

The **Eiffel Tower** gets **repainted** every **seven years.**

It's time for a change! **What color would you paint it?** Maybe it needs a new point, too.

A bridge built in **Lima, Peru,** is reportedly held together by **egg whites.**

What is your bridge made of? Make sure it won't fall apart!

Giant tube worms get energy for survival from **toxic gases.**

The deep sea is a strange and unfamiliar place, but there are ten things in this picture that would not be found under the sea. Once you find them, add whatever you would imagine is living deep in the ocean.

Deep-sea vents that spew **white particles** are called **"snowblowers."**

Some **deep-sea tube worms** have **no mouth** or **stomach.**

It was considered good luck to throw shoes at the bride and groom at 16th-century weddings in England.

ACORN
ALBATROSS
ALLIGATOR TEETH
ANKH
BAMBOO
BARN STAR
CAT'S EYE
CIRCLE
CLOVER
COIN
CRESCENT
CRICKET
CROSSING FINGERS
DOLPHIN

DRAGONFLY
DREAM CATCHER
EGGS
EYELASH
GOLDFISH
GRAPES
HAND
HORN
HORSESHOE
KEY
LADDER
LADYBUG
NORTH STAR
NUMBER SEVEN

PIG
RABBIT'S FOOT
RAINBOW
REDHEADS
SAPPHIRE
SCARAB
SHOOTING STAR
SPIDER
TIGER
TRIANGLE
TURTLE
WHEEL
WHITE ELEPHANT
WISHBONE

That sounds a little dangerous! Cross your fingers and find these good luck charms and superstitions in this word search. Words may be found horizontally, vertically, and diagonally, forward or backward. Then, ask permission to go online and research the origins of the beliefs.

```
E Y E L A S H L A D Y B U G S H D T S S
R A L L I G A T O R T E E T H R A O H H
I H S C A R A B E A H E M R A I C O E O
H S N T E E H G A T N S L G C R O F H O
P I I E A G I S L O S E O I R E R S O T
P F T K L T E R R O E N C N E D N T R I
A D O C H P E T R H F P E O S H T I O N
S L H P A D H T W L O V F O C E E B S G
T O S R I S A C Y T E R E R E A O B N S
R G G P T B V E I S E L S F N D M A I T
E R S A L I L P R R G P H E T S B R H A
E L R A N K O E A N C C A T S E Y E P R
R A T E M R B R A K H L D N A H O C L A
E D S R G M O I C I T G E E T F O R O I
V D S G U K R H B A N K H T S I D E D N
O E R N I T J T E K C I R C N Y U S T B
L R C O H P B A R N S T A R E G G S F O
C R O S S I N G F I N G E R S V Y E K W
V W H I T E E L E P H A N T O O B M A B
D R E A M C A T C H E R W I S H B O N E
```

146

Grapefruit-size hail has plummeted to Earth at a speed of **100 miles** an hour.
[161 km/h]

It once rained frogs in Kansas City, Missouri, U.S.A.

You're going to need a bigger umbrella. Create a strong and awesome-looking umbrella and some matching outer gear.

There are about a TRILLION Web pages on the Internet—that's about 140 for every person on Earth!

WWWhat wwwould your wwwebsite look like? Start with your home page. What will your URL be?

There's a **90 percent chance** your **parents will steal** some of your Halloween candy.

Help these kids find their way through this creepy cornfield without getting blocked by spooky things in their path.

START

FINISH

An architect **built a model** of the Venetian Hotel in Macau, China, using **218,792** playing cards.

Play cards! Or build something with them. Design your structure here.

ANSWERS

Page 15

A **CAVE** in Croatia has a 1,683-FOOT-DEEP PIT, the **DEEPEST HOLE** on Earth.

Time to go spelunking! Wind your way through this maze on your cave expedition.

START

FINISH

15

Page 19

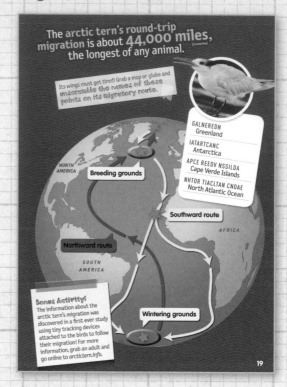

The arctic tern's round-trip migration is about **44,000 miles**, (71,000 km) the longest of any animal.

Its wings must get tired! Grab a map or globe and unscramble the names of these points on its migratory route.

GALNEREDN
Greenland

IATARTCANC
Antarctica

APCE REEDV NSSILDA
Cape Verde Islands

NHTOR TIACLTAN CNOAE
North Atlantic Ocean

NORTH AMERICA

Breeding grounds

Southward route

AFRICA

Northward route

SOUTH AMERICA

Wintering grounds

Bonus Activity!
The information about the arctic tern's migration was discovered in a first ever study using tiny tracking devices attached to the birds to follow their migration! For more information, grab an adult and go online to arctictern.info.

19

Page 23

Connect the dots to form the picture of this dog in a yoga pose.

SOME PEOPLE **PRACTICE YOGA,** OR **"DOGA,"** WITH THEIR **DOG.**

23

Page 24

The world's **LARGEST MAZE,** the Dole Pineapple Garden Maze in Hawaii, U.S.A., has **2.5 MILES** (4 km) **OF PATHS** made with **MORE THAN 14,000 PLANTS.**

Can you make your way out of this fruity maze?

START

FINISH

Page 35:
1. a; 2. c; 3. c

ANSWERS

Pages 40–41

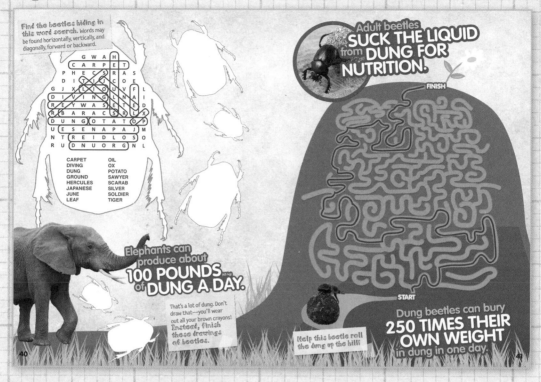

Page 43

Page 44

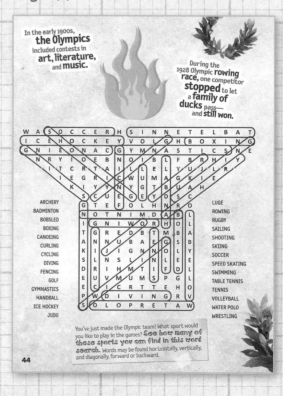

ANSWERS

Page 52

You can write about 45,000 words with an average pencil.

You can start here! Complete this crossword puzzle made up of words related to—what else?—words!

Crossword solution:
- M E S S A G E (down), ADVERB, BOOK, R (across top)
- END, DICTIONARY
- ARTICLE, NOTES
- EMAIL, POEM
- PAPER, SUBJECT
- ERASER, JOT, QUOTE

Across
2 Describes a verb or adjective
5 Last three letters of a story?
6 A book that lists words and their meanings
8 A story in a newspaper
9 Short messages, often on small pieces of paper
12 A message sent electronically
14 A piece of writing that may use 4 Down
16 A type of airplane that you can write on
18 English and math are each a ____ in school
20 Removes a pencil's mistakes
21 Quick way to write something down
22 "Repeat" another's words

Down
1 A note that might be on a board
3 An educational place for a worm?
4 "Time," "lime," and "grime" are words that ____
7 A book of synonyms
10 What has a beginning, a middle, and an end?
11 A soup with letters
13 A, B, or C
15 Secret messages that need to be deciphered
16 Group of words that isn't a full sentence
17 This special bird carried secret messages for soldiers in World War I
19 Written words in a book

52

Page 54

There are 190-million-year-old dinosaur footprints near Moab, Utah, U.S.A.

FINISH

This dino mom needs to get back to her nest! Help her find the right path to it.

START

54

Page 57

NASA's Hubble telescope captured an image of a galaxy cluster that looks like a smiley face.

Connect these dots to form the constellation Leo.

Bonus Activity!
Grab an adult and go to *spaceplace.nasa.gov/voyager-to-stars/en*. See if you can guess the sounds on the recordings carried aboard the Voyagers 1 and 2 spacecraft as they explore our star system and beyond. What message would you send to aliens who might live outside our solar system?

57

Page 62

To be, or not to be: That is the question.

Double, double toil and trouble;
Fire burn, and cauldron bubble.

There's daggers in men's smiles.

Friends, Romans, countrymen, lend me your ears.

Good night, good night! Parting is such sweet sorrow, that I shall say good night till it be morrow.

ANSWERS

Page 65

Some ORCHIDS smell like DEAD MICE.

Follow your nose and find the strong-smelling things in this word search. Words may be found horizontally, vertically, and diagonally, forward or backward.

BAD BREATH   FEET   PERFUME   TRASH
BODY ODOR   FISH   SKUNK   VOMIT
CHEESE   GARLIC SOUR MILK
COFFEE   MOLD   SWEAT
EGG   ONIONS TAR

```
T R A S   B O D Y O D O R   T
      T E E F F O C K
    H J G A R L I A
    R D G T I M O Y C
      B A D B R E A T H
    O E M U F R E P E
    S N O I N O N O E
    H S A F I T A E W S
    W E K N U K S P E
```

65

Page 74

African lions catch about 25 percent of the prey they chase.

```
          L S   S W A J
        L   T E M R E       T
    T   E N A L I E C   N O O I
    C E   S U R C M T L   S N O
    H S U   F H T A I E   O L A S
    A F K L   L T E C D V   A T
    R G C I E   N E R S   A T
    G E I D A E D Y A L   P
    E C Y K I P T   H G I   C
      Y   S L L I U Q   C
```

Word prey! Hunt for these words related to predators and prey. Don't let anyone sneak up and surprise you while you're working! Words may be found horizontally, vertically, and diagonally, forward or backward.

CHARGE   HUNT   QUILLS
CLAWS   JAWS   SMELL
CRUSH   KICK   SPEED
DETER   MIMIC   STARTLE
FIGHT   PLAY DEAD TALON
FLEE   POISON   TENTACLES

Bonus Activity!
After you circle all of the words, unscramble the unused letters to discover the shocking way that some animals attack their prey.

E L E C T R I C I T Y

74

Page 85

Your BRAIN can hold 100 TIMES MORE INFORMATION than a COMPUTER.

That's a lot of brainpower! Put it to work on this brain game.

MESSAGES from your brain TRAVEL along YOUR NERVES at up to 200 MILES an hour.
(322 km/h)

START

EMOTION
TOUCH
TEMPERATURE
HI! HOLA! BONJOUR!
LANGUAGE
SMELL
SIGHT
HEARING
COORDINATION
BREATHING
END

85

Page 86–87

Crickets detect sound through their knees.

The ancient Egyptians trained monkeys to dance and play music.

Honeybees can be trained to detect explosives.

Earthworms have five hearts.

Vision uses one third of all your brainpower.

ANSWERS

Page 88

A silkworm uses about a HALF MILE (0.8 km) of SPIT to build its COCOON.

Help this silkworm make its way to the mulberry leaf.

START

FINISH

88

Page 93

Some **three million SUNKEN SHIPS** lie on the ocean floor.

Let's go on a treasure hunt! Find the ten hidden treasures on this ship.

93

Pages 100–101

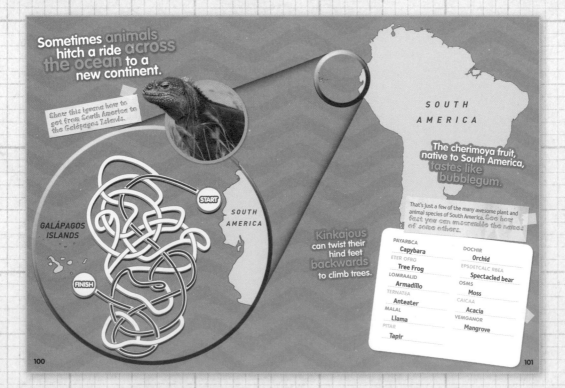

Sometimes animals hitch a ride across the ocean to a new continent.

Show this iguana how to get from South America to the Galápagos Islands.

START

GALÁPAGOS ISLANDS

SOUTH AMERICA

FINISH

Kinkajous can twist their hind feet backwards to climb trees.

100

SOUTH AMERICA

The cherimoya fruit, native to South America, tastes like bubblegum.

That's just a few of the many awesome plant and animal species of South America. See how fast you can unscramble the names of some others.

PAYARBCA **Capybara**	DOCHIR **Orchid**
ETER OFRG **Tree Frog**	EPSDETCALC RBEA **Spectacled bear**
LOMRAALID **Armadillo**	OSMS **Moss**
TERNATEA **Anteater**	CAICAA **Acacia**
MALAL **Llama**	VEMGANOR **Mangrove**
PITAR **Tapir**	

101

ANSWERS

Page 106

Page 115

HELLO

Page 117

Page 123

ANSWERS

Page 128

Page 131

Page 136–137

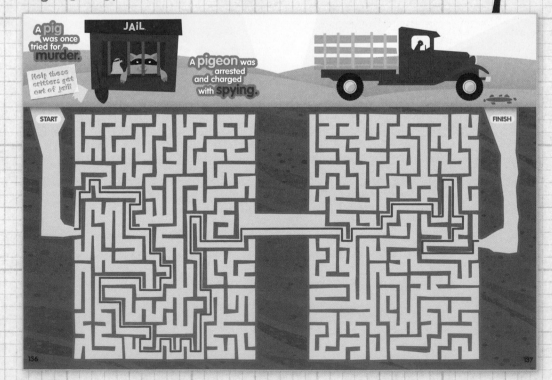

ANSWERS

Page 140

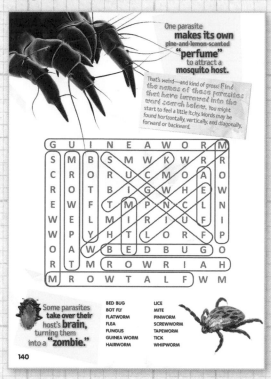

One parasite **makes its own** pine-and-lemon-scented **"perfume"** to attract a **mosquito host.**

That's weird—and kind of gross! Find the names of these parasites that have burrowed into the word search below. You might start to feel a little itchy. Words may be found horizontally, vertically, and diagonally, forward or backward.

Some parasites **take over their** host's **brain,** turning them into a **"zombie."**

BED BUG
BOT FLY
FLATWORM
FLEA
FUNGUS
GUINEA WORM
HAIRWORM

LICE
MITE
PINWORM
SCREWWORM
TAPEWORM
TICK
WHIPWORM

Page 145

The deep sea is a strange and unfamiliar place, but there are ten things in this picture that would not be found under the sea. Once you find them, add whatever you would imagine is living deep in the ocean.

Giant tube worms get energy for survival from **toxic gases.**

Deep-sea vents that spew **white particles** are called **"snowblowers."**

Some **deep-sea tube worms** have **no mouth** or **stomach.**

Page 146

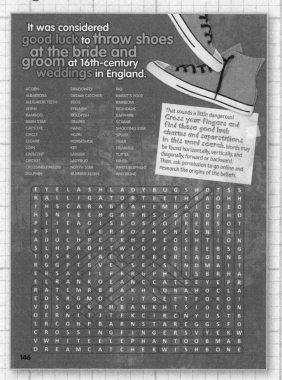

It was considered **good luck to throw shoes** at the bride and groom at 16th-century **weddings** in England.

ACORN
ALBATROSS
ALLIGATOR TEETH
ANKH
BAMBOO
BARN STAR
CAT'S EYE
CIRCLE
CLOVER
COIN
CRESCENT
CRICKET
CROSSING FINGERS
DOLPHIN

DRAGONFLY
DREAM CATCHER
EGGS
EYELASH
GOLDFISH
GRAPES
HAND
HORN
HORSESHOE
KEY
LADDER
LADYBUG
NORTH STAR
NUMBER SEVEN

PIG
RABBIT'S FOOT
RAINBOW
REDHEADS
SAPPHIRE
SCARAB
SHOOTING STAR
SPIDER
TIGER
TRIANGLE
TURTLE
WHEEL
WHITE ELEPHANT
WISHBONE

That sounds a little dangerous! Cross your fingers and find these good luck charms and superstitions in this word search. Words may be found horizontally, vertically, and diagonally, forward or backward. Then, ask permission to go online and research the origins of the beliefs.

Page 150

There's a **90 percent chance** your **parents will steal** some of your **Halloween candy.**

Help these kids find their way through this creepy cornfield without getting blocked by spooky things in their path.

CREDITS

For Kirsten and Danny, whose curiosity and creativity have always inspired me, and Rick, my number one fan.—J.G.

Word searches and crosswords created by Julie K. Cohen

Illustrations by Kevin McFadin unless otherwise noted

DRMS=Dreamstime.com; GI=Getty Images; SS=Shutterstock

FRONT COVER: (frog), Mat Hayward/SS; (lion cubs), Eric Isselée/SS; (clownfish), Kletr/SS; (piglet), Steshkin Yevgeniy/SS; (doodles), blue67design/SS; (pencil lines), Brosko/SS; **SPINE:** (frog), Mat Hayward/SS; **BACK COVER:** (dog), Fly_dragonfly/SS; (crocodile), Robert Eastman/SS; (robots), lattesmile/SS

INTERIOR: (tape pieces throughout), rzarek/SS; 2 (UP), Alex Mustard/Nature Picture Library; 2 (LO), Derek Meijer/Alamy; 2-3 (CTR), Eduard Kyslynskyy/SS; 3 (UP), aastock/SS; 3 (RT), jaroslava V/SS; 3 (LO), Four Oaks/SS; 4 (UP), SS; 4 (CTR), juan carlos tinjaca/SS; 4 (LO), bogdan ionescu/SS; 5 (CTR), MeeKo/SS; 5 (RT), javarman/SS; 7 (UP LE), Nejron Photo/SS; 7 (UP RT), djem/SS; 7 (CTR), Mana Photo/SS; 7 (CTR LE), Rich Carey/SS; 7 (LO RT), gualtiero boffi/SS; 7 (LO LE), pandapaw/SS; 9, BMJ/SS; 10 (all Legos), Mark Thiessen, NGS; 10 (lettering), Magicvector/SS; 11 (UP), Volodymyr Krasyuk/iStock/GI; 11 (LO), Steshkin Yevgeniy/SS; 12, S. D. Biju, Systematics Lab; 14, Fisherss/SS; 16 (background), Wikimedia Commons; 16 (LO), Bob Thomas/Popperfoto/GI; 17, Louisville Mega Cavern; 19, Kevin Schafer/Minden Pictures; 22 (LE), Matt Propert/NGS; 22 (RT), Diriye/iStockphoto/GI; 24, Dana Edmunds/Design Pics/Corbis; 25, Masayoshi Kanoh/REX SS; 26-27, Jeff Mauritzen/NGS; 26 (LO), Masa Ushioda/age fotostock RM/GI; 27 (LO), AP Photo/Lefteris Pitarakis; 28, Zoologische Staatssammlung Muenchen/Joern Koehler/Reuters; 30, jaroslava V/SS; 31 (UP LE), Yanta/DRMS; 31 (UP CTR), Jak Wonderly/NGS; 31 (UP RT), Ilya Akinshin/SS; 31 (LO), cbimages/Alamy; 32 (UP LE), Yoji Okata/Nature Production/Minden Pictures; 32 (UP RT), Steven Hunt/Stone Sub/GI; 32 (LO), Bridgeman Images; 33, iStock.com/MR1805; 34 (LE), Piotr Naskrecki/Minden Pictures; 34 (RT), Brandon Cole; 35, jackhollingsworth/SS; 36, PjrStudio/Alamy; 38, Wikimedia Commons; 39 (UP), CWA Studios/SS; 39 (LO), Caters News/zumapress.com/Newscom; 40, Four Oaks/SS; 41 (UP), efendy/SS; 41 (LO), efendy/SS; 43 (UP), Racheal Grazias/SS; 43 (LO), Racheal Grazias/SS; 44-45, andersphoto/SS; 47 (LE), javarman/SS; 47 (RT), Leksele/SS; 48 (LE), Brian Kubicki, Costa Rica Amphibian Research Center; 48 (RT), Mark Smith/Science Source; 49, Jodi Cobb/National Geographic Creative; 50, NASA; 53, Nick Garbutt/Corbis; 54, Franco Tempesta/NGS; 55, Jan Hinsch/Science Source; 56 (background), daboost/iStockphoto/GI; 56, Raytags/DRMS;57, NASA & ESA Acknowledgment: Judy Schmidt (geckzilla.org); 58, U.S. Navy photo by Mass Communication Specialist 3rd Class Edward Guttierrez III/Released; 61 (LE), Eric Isselée/SS; 61 (CTR), Kalmatsuy/SS; 61 (RT), Susan Schmitz/SS; 62 (UP), Melinda Fawver/SS; 62 (LO), Bangor University, UK; 63, Cultura RM/Jamel Toppin/GI; 66, Tim Laman/National Geographic Creative; 72, SS; 73, bomberclaad/GI; 74-75, G Ribiere/SS; 75 (UP), Wikimedia Commons; 75 (LO), Doug Perrine/SeaPics.com; 76, Geoff Robinson/REX SS; 79, iStock.com/Antagain; 80, Derek Meijer/Alamy; 81, Brand New Images/Iconica/GI; 83 (UP), FEATURECHINA/Newscom; 83 (LO), Danny Alvarez/SS; 84, Eric Isselée/SS; 85, CTON; 86-87, Carol M. Highsmith/Buyenlarge/GI; 86, Paisan Homhuan/SS; 87, Mike Flippo/SS; 89, Lucy Pemoni/Reuters; 90-91, NASA; 90, MeeKo/SS; 91 (inset), Joe Vogan/Alamy; 92 (UP), Sputnik Images; 92 (LO), Sputnik Images; 93, Stephen Frink/Science Faction/Corbis; 93 (sea star), Joao Virissimo/SS; 93 (sword), Viktor Kunz/SS; 93 (key), Karin Hildebrand Lau/SS; 93 (binoculars), Andrew Buckin/SS; 93 (gold coins), teena137/SS; 93 (pirate hat), VannPhotography/SS; 93 (treasure chest), Wolfilser/SS; 94, iStock.com/M. Unal Ozmene; 95 (UP LE), stockfoto-graf/SS; 95 (UP RT), Photodisc; 95 (LO LE), bogdan ionescu/SS; 95 (LO RT), pukach/SS; 96, Iakov Filimonov/SS; 97, Kevin Schafer/Minden Pictures; 98, jenifoto/iStockphoto/GI; 99 (UP), Neil Setchfield/Alamy; 99 (LO), Carlo Fiumana/iStockphoto/GI; 100, Roger De Marfà/iStockphoto/GI; 102, AP Photo/Richard Drew; 104, Yanbing Shi/Flickr RF/GI; 105 (UP), Kjell Sandved/Visuals Unlimited, Inc.; 105 (CTR), Bill Perry/SS; 105 (LO), Mariusz S. Jurgielewicz/SS; 106, Tim Fitzharris/Minden Pictures; 106 (inset), Klaus Balzano/Ge/Moment Opentty Images; 107 (UP), Scott J. Ferrell/Congressional Quarterly/Alamy; 107 (CTR LE), NASA/Goddard Space Flight Center Conceptual Image Lab; 107 (CTR RT), NASA/JPL-Caltech/MSSS/Texas A&M Univ.; 107 (LO), Steve A. Munsinger/Science Source; 109, NASA; 110 (UP), contemporary art by AKI INOMATA; 110 (LO), contemporary art by AKI INOMATA; 111, contemporary art by AKI INOMATA; 112 (dart board), Photodisc; 112 (beach ball), Olga Popova/SS; 112 (boomerang), Photodisc; 112 (stuffed monkey), Rebecca Hale, NGS; 112 (soccer ball), irin-k/SS; 112 (yellow darts), Photodisc; 112 (yellow pool ball), Vittorio Bruno/SS; 112 (hockey puck), Photodisc; 112 (pink water gun), Marc Dietrich/SS; 112 (checkers), Photodisc; 112 (jacks & ball), Photodisc; 112 (rainbow slinky), Kitchner Bain/DRMS; 112 (playing cards), Diana Valujeva/SS; 112 (toy truck), Photodisc; 112 (green die), Photodisc; 112 (chatter teeth), aastock/SS; 112 (basketball), Aaron Amat/SS; 112 (toy shark), juan carlos tinjaca/SS; 112 (dog catching Frisbee), Douglas Menuez/Riser/GI; 113 (UP), Alex Mustard/Nature Picture Library; 113 (LO), Rudie Kuiter/OceanwideImages.com; 114 (UP), University of Florida/Florida Institute of Technology/Southwest Research Institute; 114 (LO), Rick Saake/Reno Tahoe USA; 115, MeeKo/GI; 116, AP Photo/Kathy Willens; 118 (LE), Michael Nichols/National Geographic Creative; 118 (RT), Cyril Ruoso/JH Editorial/Minden Pictures; 119, Eduard Kyslynskyy/SS; 122, David Aguilar/NGS; 126, NASA/REX SS; 127, Anton_Ivanov/SS; 128, David Aguilar/NGS; 130 (UP), Juniors Bildarchiv GmbH/Alamy; 130 (CTR LE), Noelleherzog/DRMS; 130 (CTR RT), Tania Thomson/SS; 130 (LO), Super Prin/SS; 131 (UP), Albertoloyo/DRMS; 131 (CTR LE), James Michael Dor/SS; 131 (CTR RT), Ajn/DRMS; 131 (LO), Hung Chung Chih/SS; 132 (LE), Jean-Michel Girard/SS; 132 (UP RT), Ozja/SS; 132 (LO RT), Richard Nowitz/Digital Vision; 134, Trybex/SS; 135 (UP LE), Elena Schweitzer/SS; 135 (UP RT), Boule/SS; 135 (LO), Ljupco Smokovski/SS; 138 (UP LE), Roland Seitre/Nature Picture Library; 138 (UP RT), Bruce Coleman/Photoshot; 138 (LO LE), Jelly Belly Candy Company; 138 (LO RT), Jiri Hera/SS; 139, Duncan Walker/GI; 140 (UP), Sebastian Kaulitzki/SS; 140 (LO LE), Anand Varma/National Geographic Creative; 140 (LO RT), D. Kucharski K. Kucharska/SS; 141, iStock.com/Clu; 142, David Noton/NPL/Minden Pictures; 143, Pola Damonte/SS; 144 (LE), Manfred Gottschalk/Lonely Planet Images/GI; 144 (RT), muratart/SS; 145 (LE), Franco Banfi/Collection/Photoshot; 145 (RT), David Shale/npl/Minden Pictures; 146, Borislav Bajkic/SS; 151, Bobby Yip/Reuters; 152, robynmac/iStockphoto/GI; 154, Melinda Fawver/SS; 156, Kitchner Bain/DRMS; 156, Ilya Akinshin/SS; 157, Leksele/SS; 158, Yanta/DRMS

STICKER PAGE 1: (SOLD tag), Brand X; (gems), Rozaliya/DRMS; (guitar), iStock.com/acarart; (spider), Eric Isselée/SS; (ketchup & mustard), Joe Belanger/SS; (fish), Eric Isselée/SS; (orangutan), Eric Isselée/SS;

(flames), hugolacasse/SS; (push pins), Marsel82/SS; (doughnut), Bryan Solomon/SS; (car), Iaroslav Neliubov/SS; (sandwich), Davydenko Yuliia/SS; (mouse), CreativeNature R.Zwerver/SS; **STICKER PAGE 2:** (turtle), Eric Isselée/SS; (skyscraper), HomeStudio/SS; (blue ribbon), Danny E Hooks/SS; (koalas), Eric Isselée/SS; (french fries), Richard Peterson/SS; (ice cream), M. Unal Ozmen/SS; (cupcake), Darren Brode/SS; (funny face), Mira Bavutti Deganello/SS; (beetle), irin-k/SS; (crocodile), Robert Eastman/SS; (pizza), images.etc/SS; (saxophone), Vereshchagin Dmit/SS; (dog), Fly_dragonfly/SS; (dinosaur), DM7/SS; (witch hat), pukach/SS; (cat), Tony Campbell/SS; (gift), Kim Nguyen/SS; (bear), Rosa Jay/SS; (gems), Rozaliya/DRMS; (flowers), iStock.com/jurisam; (rubber duck), Photodisc; **STICKER PAGE 3:** (globe), Chin Kit Sen/SS; (magician hat & wand), SS; (kitten), Elena Butinova/SS; (school bus), Joy Brown/SS; (rocket), KamiGami/SS; (tiara), Elnur/SS; (sunscreen), Kraska/SS; (sea star), Elena Schweitzer/SS; (wizard hat), Chamille White/SS; (push pins), Marsel82/SS; (Popsicles), graja/SS; (speech bubbles), MR Gao/SS; (lightbulb), Somchai Som/SS; (hound dog), WilleeCole/SS; (blue balloon), Bo Valentino/SS; (piggy bank), Micha/SS; (beach ball), Christophe Testi/DRMS; (umbrella), Elnur/DRMS; (gems), Rozaliya/DRMS; (apple), iStock.com/rimglow; (octopus), iStock.com/Tribalium; (backpack), iStock.com/Pogonici; **STICKER PAGE 4:** (fingerprint), SS; (eye mask), SS; (graduation cap), Quang Ho/SS; (panda), Eric Isselée/SS; (rocket), KamiGami/SS; (chameleon), larus/SS; (magnifying glass), tuulijumala/SS; (round sticker), Episcons/SS; (baseball cap), Anastasios Kandris/SS; (push pins), Marsel82/SS; (elephant), Talvi/SS; (Saturn), SSSCCC/SS; (Popsicles), graja/SS; (hot-air balloon), tulpahn/SS; (astronaut), stockphoto mania/SS; (Earth), gst/SS; (speech bubbles), MR Gao/SS; (squirrel), IrinaK/SS; (Chihuahua dog), Andrey_Kuzmin/SS; (octopus toy), SS; (rain boots), Sarycheva Olesia/SS; (pencil), Tharakorn Arunothai/SS; (take-out food container), Hurst Photo/SS; (skateboard), Heike Brauer/SS; (angler fish), SketchingG/SS; (gems), Rozaliya/DRMS; (unicorn), iStock.com/walbyent; (dog wearing backpack), iStock.com/WilleeCole; (film clapper board), Photodisc

Since 1888, the National Geographic Society has funded more than 12,000 research, exploration, and preservation projects around the world. The Society receives funds from National Geographic Partners, LLC, funded in part by your purchase. A portion of the proceeds from this book supports this vital work.

For more information, visit www.natgeo.com/info, call 1-800-647-5463, or write to the following address:
National Geographic Partners, LLC
1145 17th Street N.W.
Washington, D.C. 20036-4688 U.S.A.

Visit us online at nationalgeographic.com/books

For librarians and teachers: ngchildrensbooks.org

More for kids from National Geographic:
kids.nationalgeographic.com

For information about special discounts for bulk purchases, please contact National Geographic Books Special Sales: ngspecsales@ngs.org

For rights or permissions inquiries, please contact National Geographic Books Subsidiary Rights: ngbookrights@ngs.org

NATIONAL GEOGRAPHIC and Yellow Border Design are trademarks of the National Geographic Society, used under license.

Designed by Fan Works Design LLC

Art Direction by Julide Dengel

Paperback ISBN: 978-1-4263-2456-7

Printed in China

16/PPS/1

BYE!